THE UNIVERSE ALWAYS HAS A PLAN

ALSO BY MATT KAHN

Whatever Arises, Love That

*Everything Is Here to Help You**

*Simplify Your Spiritual Path Online Course**

*The Healing Mantra Deck**

*Available from Hay House
Please visit:

Hay House India: www.hayhouse.co.in
Hay House USA: www.hayhouse.com®
Hay House Australia: www.hayhouse.com.au Hay
House UK: www.hayhouse.co.uk

Praise for

THE UNIVERSE ALWAYS HAS A PLAN

"*The Universe Always Has a Plan* is unlike anything I've seen or read before. Matt Kahn has articulated the basics of a new and more compassionate spirituality that—at last—includes our emotions and our humanity as well as our divinity. His Golden Rules are game changers that have the power to shift the way you see yourself and your world—bringing love, compassion, healing, joy, and humor—where before, there was shame, blame, and criticism. I love this book."

— **Christiane Northrup, M.D.**, *New York Times* best-selling author of *Goddesses Never Age* and *Women's Bodies, Women's Wisdom*

"*The Universe Always Has a Plan* is a beautiful book that really showcases Matt Kahn's soul sensitive work. He takes you on a journey that explores 10 powerful Golden Rules along with impactful mantras and simple exercises that will lead you on a journey of transformation, self-fulfillment, and emotional freedom—creating a life of joy and purpose. I highly recommend this book for anyone regardless of where they are on their spiritual journey."

— **Anita Moorjani**, *New York Times* best-selling author of *Dying to Be Me* and *What if This is Heaven?*

"When you read truths like those contained in this book, they seem so clear, so obvious, and so liberating, that you can never unknow them again. In this way, Matt Kahn delivers us, once again, to the sanity of a love-based life, compassionately busting all of the reflexive myths that have kept us stuck in suffering."

— **Kelly Brogan, M.D.**, holistic psychiatrist and *New York Times* best-selling author of *A Mind of Your Own* and *Own Your Self*

THE UNIVERSE ALWAYS HAS A PLAN

The 10 Golden Rules of Letting Go

MATT KAHN

HAY HOUSE

HAY HOUSE INDIA

New Delhi • London • Sydney
Carlsbad, California • New York City

Hay House Publishers (India) Pvt Ltd
Muskaan Complex, Plot No. 3, B-2, Vasant Kunj, New Delhi – 110 070, India

Hay House LLC, P.O. Box 5100, Carlsbad, CA 92018-5100, USA
Hay House UK Ltd, The Sixth Floor, Watson House, 54 Baker Street, London W1U 7BU, UK
Hay House Australia Publishing Pty Ltd, 18/36 Ralph St., Alexandria NSW 2015, Australia

Email: contact@hayhouse.co.in
Website: www.hayhouse.co.in

Cover design: Mary Ann Smith
Interior design: Nick C. Welch

First published by Hay House India, 2023
Reprint, 2026
20 19 18 17 16 15 14 13 12 11

ISBN 978-93-94613-43-0

Printed at Repro India Limited

MIX
Paper from responsible sources
FSC® C047271
FSC www.fsc.org

Hay House is committed to a sustainable future for our business, our readers and our planet. This book is made from Forest Stewardship Council® certified paper.

CONTENTS

INTRODUCTION

You've reached a turning point in your reality. A moment in time when the things that used to hold your interest fail to provide the comfort they once did. You may not know where things are headed, but you can clearly sense *a withering away* of how things used to be. It's a time of transformation, where the dissolving of relationships or roles makes room for new experiences to be birthed. It is much like a spiritual form of empty nest syndrome, a time of big change and loss.

Do you feel an insatiable drive to fulfill a mission greater than yourself? To be reacquainted with a long-lost desire to follow the excitement of passion, inspiration, and playfulness? As this happens, you can start to feel the walls of your conditioned mindset crumble.

Liberation has knocked on your door, and perhaps for the first time in your history, something within you has chosen to open to its request before even knowing what awaits on the other side.

You may not know where you'll be headed, but trust me when I tell you: it can only get better from here. It might seem scary, but *nothing* can stop you from taking the leap.

This is the emergence of life's highest purpose: the birthing of a spiritually fueled reality. It's time to let go, and leap, as a miraculous new world takes shape around you.

We have been brought together in this book for that very reason—to take these next exciting steps forward into a new world brimming with the joy of emotional freedom that only letting go can provide.

No matter the circumstances you currently face, the solution to each question, concern, or existential crisis is letting go. In order to help you let go with as much peace and ease as possible, I am sharing with you the wisdom to help you find the light throughout life's darkest tunnels.

By learning how to truly let go and be emotionally free, you maximize your infinite joy and fulfillment in a way that resonates with the details and demands of your modern-day world. You thrive in the presence of change. The mystery of outcome excites you instead of overwhelming you. Your passion invigorates you, and you act upon courageous decisions with unwavering clarity. You have more natural patience and compassion for yourself and others. You are empathically in tune with other people's experiences, while being aware of what is and isn't a part of *your* experience. The infinite current of unconditional love nourishes your heart. It allows you to *flow* with reality, instead of attempting to *control* it. As you let go into the grace of emotional freedom, you are finally able to feel so effortlessly connected *at all times* to the Universe's plan for you. These are the magnificent milestones that become your personal testimony of life on planet Earth.

In this book, I'll be sharing a set of divinely curated Universal truths, known as the 10 Golden Rules. They are here to guide you into a new dimension of human existence. Each Golden Rule will assist you through this mesmerizing process of transformation.

Everyday life doesn't stop, I know. You still have bills to pay, deadlines to meet, commitments to keep, and ambitions you'd love more time and space to fulfill. The last thing you need added to your plate are more spiritual problems to solve!

It is my great honor to share the 10 Golden Rules to help you let go—to enter the timeless joy of emotional freedom—in a way that fits into the details and demands of your modern-day reality.

Along with each Golden Rule, there'll be exercises and mantras that I will give to help you explore each attribute of your highest potential in the most practical way. Each chapter will also highlight personal stories of how each Golden Rule has been implemented throughout my life. I will serve as your resident "spiritual myth buster," helping you see through the facade of superstitious beliefs and limited viewpoints, to lead you into a more heart-centered reality.

As we begin, I thank you for your openness and trust in taking this journey with me.

GOLDEN RULE #1

YOU'VE DONE NOTHING WRONG

When I was a child, I was taught how to determine right from wrong by the reactions of others. While this helped me develop an inner compass of empathy, it also raised me to perceive life from a rather co-dependent viewpoint. Whether it was being afraid of upsetting my parents, getting on Santa's naughty list, or even a fear of disappointing God, I learned to measure the validity of my choices by how much pleasure or how little pain it caused other people. As I became older, I began growing out of this co-dependent mind-set, no longer willing to live imprisoned by being "all things to all people." I saw how devoting my life to helping others avoid pain had failed to provide me with the pleasure of acceptance, which only I could give to myself. I also saw how other people's adverse reactions to the choices that were useful for me couldn't cause them any tangible pain outside of their judgments.

I inevitably learned that while it's useful to consider other people's experiences, ultimately, their reactions couldn't indicate how aligned or misaligned I was. This useful line I drew in the sand would be so clearly demonstrated in my relationship with my mom. Growing up, I wouldn't dare do anything to upset her, primarily because I was conditioned to seek the reward of her love.

Year after year, I either noticed much of my good behavior going unnoticed, or more precisely, the eruptions of my mom's ego coming from her lack of patience or degree of stress, with no actual relationship between my actions and her view of experience. I began to see how much of my mom's life upset her. It wasn't just me; it was servers at restaurants, her boss, my dad, my sister, her countless hours of volunteer work at the local temple, and even people in traffic.

This helped me see how frustrated, disempowered, overworked, and underappreciated my mom was as the source of her discontent, merely masquerading as a response to *my* behavior. It was useless to walk on eggshells around her. I came to see the beautiful woman who birthed me into the world was deeply unhappy regardless of my actions. This was where I began to align my choices with those that supported *my* well-being, instead of relying on others as a clear mirror of reflection. I was becoming a mirror unto myself and making great strides in overcoming the co-dependent patterns of my childhood.

Such strides became rather obvious as I grew up and had the chance to introduce my mom to her adult son. Up until that point, my mom was my greatest supporter, unless the value of my choices triggered the disapproval of her abandonment issues. I remember telling my mom I was moving from California to Washington to start my career as a spiritual teacher. I could see in my mom's face the pain of having a child move so far away and how much space that would create for her loneliness to grow.

While my mom's emotions didn't prevent me from doing what I knew in my heart was right for my journey, like an obedient son, I made many promises to call often and visit her, in order to keep the approval I had spent my childhood relying on for validation, safety, and comfort.

Eventually, there came times when I missed holiday gatherings due to tour schedules, which gave me the opportunity to face my mom's disapproval and unintentionally manipulative behavior yet again, head on. Her once threatening words of disapproval and projections of selfishness became cries for the love she relied on from others, that she had no interest at that point in giving herself. Eventually, a series of insurmountable health scares would lead my mom to learning how to love herself and embrace the teachings of my first book, *Whatever Arises, Love That.*

It also transformed our relationship into a very heart-centered bond of trust, equality, and respect, which couldn't have been established unless I was willing to see how my actions aren't always the cause of someone's feelings. It was at this point in my life where I truly embraced the wisdom of the first Golden Rule: *"You've done nothing wrong."*

This rule is one of the core tenets of spiritual mastery. In order to master the art of letting go, Golden Rule #1 acts as the go-to statement we always go back to, whenever in doubt.

Even though it is common for the mind to want to jump in with the most despicable life examples to contradict its wisdom, just feel into it for a moment. What is it like to sit with the knowledge that you've done nothing wrong, no matter what others may insist to be true? On an emotional level, even if only a small percentage of you can consider its validity, how does it feel to contemplate you've done nothing wrong?

Just as you have grown from an infant to a child and then from a child to an adult, so too is your level of consciousness evolving from one spectrum of perception to another. What may have seemed true when you were younger may seem wildly fanciful in adulthood. This didn't make it wrong to think and perceive as you did when you were younger, simply because it took all your experiences in childhood to inspire the growth the "adult you" holds to be true. In the same way, the Universe doesn't require you to spin your wheels trying to apologize for a past that played out exactly as it was meant to be. This is the incredible evidence of a spiritual journey every human being has been navigating since the moment they were born.

If you're in a physical body, you're on a spiritual journey. Some people might tell you they're not "into spirituality." Truth be told, we're all on a spiritual journey because we exist. Throughout this journey, you will see life one way and then you will have an expansion causing you to see life differently. I'm sure you've had this experience, where, in retrospect, you wonder, "Why didn't I think of that? In the moment, how come I didn't see it that way?" No matter how hard you work to know life lessons ahead of time, you are always going to see each moment from the highest level of consciousness available to you. However any moment is seen will cause you to expand to a higher level of consciousness that will then show you later what you didn't see before.

As the main theme in my book *Everything Is Here to Help You,* the spiritual journey is a transition out of ego and into the soul. This means in every moment, we can either see from the ego's perspective or from the soul's perspective. If we see life from the ego's point of view, we are bound to view life through the eyes of regret. From this perspective, we are led to think: "Since I now know what I didn't know before, I regret that I didn't have this perception then." When you regret, the tendency is to *blame*. More than likely, you've only developed a tendency to blame because you've experienced being blamed yourself.

What the ego regrets in outcome, the soul rejoices in opportunity. The soul says, *"Yes, I now know more than I knew before and how great that I had to live out that moment. I had to see it the way it was meant to be seen. I had to be who I needed to be. I needed to do everything that needed to happen in order to get to this moment where I've been gifted now with a greater perspective."*

Contrary to the soul's perspective, the ego thinks, *"Oh my god, I now see it differently than I did before, and I wish I could've seen it that way all along."* In order to keep itself well fed by inner judgment and self-criticism, the ego views itself through a lens of faults and flaws. From this standpoint, life is a punishment and a curse, instead of a gift and a blessing. Beyond the negative self-talk of the ego's perspective, the soul honors the expanded viewpoint that you now have as life's way of rewarding you for surviving a moment exactly the way it was designed. You survived a moment playing exactly the character life asked you to play. You did and said every single thing that life asked you to do and say, and the reward is a greater perspective that frees you from the need to be that version of a character ever again.

It is this very gift of perspective the soul rejoices that remains a vital part of a miraculous plan the Universe always has for you.

To further the healing perpetuated by self-blame, imagine a moment in your life where your behavior was the most regrettable. Notice how from the ego's perspective, any tendency to feel embarrassed or ashamed of how you acted during this time. Simply take a few breaths to allow your body to be a space of relaxation that gives these uncomfortable feelings a safe place to land. As the shock and awe of embarrassment begins to fade, can you sense within you a deeper cosmic order to life that only had you play out the very words and actions to inspire a series of expansions that made you who you are right now? If you are able to look back on the past, aware of wisdom you didn't have at the time, then the journey from that memory to the present time has undoubtedly served you well. Equally so, can you begin to accept how everything you needed to say and do to become who you are now is the exact circumstance others required to be who they are today?

Whether you are able to give yourself a much-needed break from self-criticism, or at least make more peace with how life was meant to play out, you are taking an exciting step forward. Whether you believe you did nothing wrong or not, the fact remains, no amount of regret can reshape the past that is only here to serve you.

SHIFTING OUT OF REGRET

In order to realize the truth of "You did nothing wrong," we need to use self-compassion, one of the soul's attributes, to shift out of regret and into rejoicing. Self-compassion is the ability to be easy with yourself. It is the opposite of harshness. It is a moment of growth that requires no punishment, condemnation, or criticism, in order to learn from anyone's actions. No matter how harsh of a world you feel you live in, no matter how ruthless of a past you may have endured, self-compassion says, "Can you just take one moment and be the nicest, most supportive and open-minded person that you are encountering right now?" Can you meet yourself as an ally instead of an enemy? Can you turn inward and say to yourself, "Hello, friend, how can I be here for you?"

Have you ever, in the midst of stress or turmoil, encountered a fresh breath of kind and attentive customer service, where someone just went a little bit out of their way to make sure that you were comfortable, served, and cared for?

Self-compassion is when you are that attentive to *yourself.* Self-compassion begins with accepting that you don't have to necessarily know exactly what's right about every moment of your life, but beginning with Golden Rule #1, you certainly know that you've done nothing wrong.

There is no doubt that you're going to be better and better and better than you've ever been before, but that doesn't mean that the way you were in the past was wrong. Simply because, in order to get to this stage of evolution, you and everyone else had to be *exactly* the way they were. From this perspective, every gift of expansion is life thanking you for playing the exact role in every person's life, whether or not you were the most popular person in the room or even likable in your own experience.

All too often, the ego believes if you are not the most popular person in the room, you must be doing something wrong. Most likely because you've been trained to be fueled by the validation and approval of others. How many times have you felt that if someone else in your life doesn't agree with you, you're wrong? Contrary to this people-pleasing mechanism, Golden Rule #1 helps you see if someone doesn't agree with you, it could only be because you both are on two different paths. If someone insists you should go right, but you know in your heart to go left, maybe this is where your paths take you both in different directions. Maybe we are walking together but not all following the same pathways home. Maybe we're just accompanying one another, for as long as we're meant to be, because we're all going in the direction of our highest potential, which doesn't always lead us in the same direction.

The reason you are reading these words is because you are on a heart-centered path. A path that says, "I don't have to imagine that I've done something wrong, grovel and beg for forgiveness from the Universe like I'm projecting parental qualities onto my own divinity. I can rejoice in my learning and grow *without* regretting. I can expand and shine *without* blaming myself. In any given moment, what I chose to do was not a flaw or a human limitation at play. Instead, it was the absolute perfection of divinity getting me to a more expanded vibrational alignment by having me play a character who only appeared to do a series of imperfect things to have experiences I would learn from."

As you may already be starting to realize, it is *impossible* to see what is right in your reality if you spend time focusing on the things that you've done wrong. While the ego may perceive this Golden Rule as a bypass of self-responsibility, there is nothing to avert, avoid, or overlook at all. Because the ego perceives through beliefs of reward and punishment, it insists you must punish yourself, if others report harm or wrongdoing as a result of your choices.

Just because you've done nothing wrong, it doesn't mean *others* are wrong for having their own perceptions of experience. You might not have done anything wrong, but neither has anyone else. Through the eyes of the Universe, you don't need to project wrongdoing on yourself and others in order to offer the gift of forgiveness. In fact, the transformative power of forgiveness is prevented from healing your past and the atrocities of other people's experiences when bumping up against the ego's categories of right versus wrong.

There may very well be experiences that have happened to you where the choices others made were categorically opposite to the ethics and values of your consciousness. There may be feelings of unfairness; feelings of being taken advantage of; anger toward perpetrators; or resentment against those who didn't listen, believe, or act assertively in your defense. Whether due to betrayal, neglect, or abuse, it is not wrong to feel exactly the way you do. While I am here outlining the trajectory of healing that each moment of pain inspires, I would ask you to be easy with yourself, offering the gift of self-compassion that reminds you, "You may forgive at some point, but it doesn't have to be today, next week, or even in the foreseeable future."

True forgiveness occurs as a result of free will. Often times it is giving yourself the right to not forgive that loosens the ego's inner grip of protection that allows forgiveness to be offered from a more authentic space. Forgiveness isn't a matter of saying any betrayal, neglect, or abuse was deserving. It's a matter of acknowledging that those who have made an indelible impression upon your history have only set you in a direction toward the arrival of your highest destiny. It's very easy to say thank you for the pleasurable experiences others provide, but it's an entirely different paradigm to slowly move in the direction of authentically thanking everyone for their contribution in your journey—even when their actions were the opposite of the love and safety your innocence wanted and needed.

Such a level of unconditional love exists outside the domain of ego, so it's natural for such a Golden Rule to merely remind you where you are in your journey. Since you've done nothing wrong, it isn't wrong or unjust to refuse forgiveness for the actions of others. You must have the right to withhold forgiveness in order to build up the courage to offer it. Once offered, you will see how a willingness to forgive unconscionable actions helps you transcend the entire cycle of victimhood. As this occurs, it helps to reform your perpetrator on an energetic level to ensure no one else may be harmed. You can think of the word *forgiving* to mean "thank you for giving me the opportunity to act from a greater level of awareness than the unconsciousness that hurt me."

This reminds me of the first time I glimpsed this depth of wisdom. I was sitting in my living room sometime in my thirties, contemplating the true meaning of forgiveness. At that moment, I was flooded with visions of my past: from scenes of being yelled at by my parents, to moments of being bullied in middle school, even beat up on a few occasions for the sheer amusement of others. Usually such images would inspire frustration, anger, humiliation, pain, and a sense of unfairness, but this time I saw them from a much different standpoint. It was as if I were witnessing it from a distance, like someone in a movie theater viewing the life and times of a main character. As I reviewed all of the people who had wronged me, I began seeing each moment of hurt as a setup of greater evolution. I saw how I had been chosen by the Universe to play the role of the victim, just as each of them had been cast in the role of the victimizer. I saw so clearly how we had each intersected one another's paths in order to come out the other end more healed, expanded, and evolved than we were before. My role was to have every reason to harbor grudges within my logical mind, with endless justifications as to why it was only fair to label and condemn each character as an enemy. This would be the very belief I would be given the chance to surrender, including the notion of being vulnerable to future attacks if my ego's job wasn't to constantly stand guard.

I saw that by forgiving each character, I was instilling in myself an even higher vibration of consciousness than the impulses that caused others to mistreat and harm me. In doing so, I sent waves of energy throughout the cosmos to be delivered into their energy fields to inspire deeper emotional resolve. I saw how my willingness to forgive made each character more heart-centered over the course of their lifetime to decrease the likelihood that anyone else in their life, including themselves, would be harmed in any way.

From this standpoint, I felt less like a person wronged by others and more like one of their guardian angels. I was merely playing a character they wronged for the chance to give the gift of consciousness. When seeing myself from this perspective, how I had the opportunity to give the greatest gift of healing to those who inflicted the most pain onto me, something collapsed in my mind. I was no longer hindered or limited by beliefs in fairness or any "eye for an eye" mentality. Instead, I rejoiced in my willingness to be *bigger* than the pain and persecution I felt by giving to another exactly what they needed to grow beyond the desire to hurt others as a result of their unresolved wounds.

In this vision, I was acting as the Universe in form, instead of from a belief in being a character who needed others to hurt for the pain they caused. While wrongdoing had been done to me, no one had to be shamed or condemned in order for each of our hearts to be set free. Instead of this moment of radical forgiveness bringing more abusers into my reality, it actually became the moment when all of life seemed to conspire to support me in miraculous ways. In a way that could never make sense to my rational mind, I didn't attract abusive encounters because I did something wrong. It occurred to usher me into a depth of transcendent forgiveness I am so grateful I was ready to accept. In being willing to forgive the seemingly unforgivable, I transcended the cycle of victimhood, which has since that moment rendered me free from perpetrators and abusers, now that forgiveness has become instinctive.

No matter the depth of hurt, forgiveness energetically heals emotional wounds, transforming perpetrators and victims into heroes. Sometimes, it is the actions of the legal system that create the breaking point in someone's unconsciousness to allow something deeper to shine through. You may very well be motivated to follow through with legal recourse to ensure the unconscious actions of one person do not harm another, while spiritually cleansing your soul of any degree of darkness through acts of radical forgiveness.

If your history of pain is way more intense than my personal example, I wholeheartedly honor the even deeper opportunity you've been given to ascend into higher realms of consciousness through the forgiveness you have a chance to offer. With the utmost compassion and respect for the circumstances you've survived, the greater the pain or displacement any egregious act instills provides an equal amount of cosmic relief for those who forgive instead of fight. Even if you cannot see beyond the confines of your inner grudge, it sometimes requires steadfast commitment in battling with the past to create enough pressure for truths of a higher level to blossom within you.

If self-compassion is the attribute cultivated in Golden Rule #1, then forgiveness is a willingness to show equal compassion to *all* hearts, no matter the roles anyone plays. If this seems too far-reaching, just remember the wording of the first Golden Rule: "*You have done nothing wrong.*" Nothing in that sentence suggests the existence of others; therefore, in the beginning, there is no reason to consider whether no one else but you has done anything wrong.

As a rule of thumb, always be the first recipient of your self-compassion and allow forgiveness to spread out on its own time frame.

YOUR MANTRA FOR RULE #1

To begin the process of infusing yourself with more self-compassion, please repeat the following statement out loud.

In order to be who I was born to become,
life couldn't have happened
any other way.

Take a deep breath and see how it feels to embrace a depth of acceptance beyond anything the ego can believe.

In order to be who I was born to become,
life couldn't have happened
any other way.

Just feel that for a moment.

Life couldn't have happened any other way. Even though you have choice in every moment, your choice is simply to reflect back to the Universe the level of consciousness you're currently operating from. In order to be who you're born to become, life couldn't have happened any other way. Translation: you did nothing wrong. Even just the consideration of this truth creates the cultivation of self-compassion. This is because only self-compassion can hear its depth of meaning. Only self-compassion can agree with this. Equally so, only the ego can disagree. Only the ego can hear you've done nothing wrong and say, I beg to differ. No matter how harsh, opinionated, or narrow-minded your inner critic seems to be, it is always important to have great humility and compassion for the ego. Like a precocious little child, its purpose is to remember your history of experiences to ensure each one inspires the healing and transformation it was created to provide. Through the eyes of the Universe, there are equal amounts of compassion for all, which allows you to become sincerely endeared by the ego instead of upset by it.

Let's take it even deeper. If you've done nothing wrong, *neither has your ego.* How deep is that? I say this because on the spiritual path, how many times have you gotten to the point of it being like, "Oh well, yeah, I can get into the alignment with my soul in my private meditation practice, in my yoga practice, and at spiritual events, and then there are these people, places, and things that trigger me." In a modern-day spiritual journey, you walk around almost like a member of the ego police. Maybe you've had these conversations where you go back and forth, tattle-telling on your ego to others.

When you're one foot out of the ego and one foot into the soul, you're aware of your conditioned behavior, but it's experienced as an ego that's horrified by itself. This is how blame and regret come into play. All too often, instead of judging others, we just turn judgment onto ourselves. It can actually be very painful. This is why you need great compassion, love, and heart-centered kindness. In the process of doing deep spiritual work, you can harm yourself just as much as someone else can. I would like to absolve you of that. You can certainly be better, grow from your experiences, and evolve as a result. But you do not have to punish yourself along the way. Karma is not a predestined jail sentence. It is not a debt you have to pay back. Karma, either negative or positive, is simply the things you say to yourself in response to what happens. Any form of negative karma is merely the tendency to say unkind things to yourself as a result of being the character you don't want to be. When you don't have to punish yourself, even for the things you think are punishing you—karmic patterns begin to heal.

How many times have you asked yourself, "Why am I attracting this?" You're attracting this because the soul's evolution is about building unconditionally loving relationships with all parts of yourself represented as each emotion. In order to grow out of the ego's swirl of regret and graduate into the vibration of rejoicing, it is *essential* to cultivate self-compassion in response to any particular outcome. This means things will happen just so you can say to yourself, "I've done nothing wrong." You will manifest experiences that might even embarrass your ego, just for the opportunity to say, "In order to be who I was born to become, life couldn't have happened any other way."

Once there is nothing that can happen in life to prevent the receiving of self-compassion, or restrict the offering of forgiveness, there is no further wisdom for adversity to teach you.

EXERCISE: Your Spiritual Evolution

Think of all of the things in your life that you think you did wrong. What are the things you hold against yourself?

Let's unravel the case you have against you. What are the things that when you pass through the gates of heaven you might think, "I hope we don't talk about *that*."

Could it be possible that the things you think you've done wrong were actually exactly right for your highest evolution? How were the things you did wrong actually right for you?

Take a moment to openly consider it.

If that feels like a moment of relief, you're one step closer to letting go. If not, only more self-compassion is needed.

SPIRITUAL MYTH-BUSTING: "Life happens as a result of my vibration."

When you embrace the wisdom of Golden Rule #1, it helps you dispel old myths that suggest the outcomes and circumstances of life occur as a reflection of your vibrational frequency. Nothing could be more disempowering than to endure the hardship of loss, change, abuse, betrayal, and neglect, only to then judge yourself as being low on the spiritual totem pole. While the ego attempts to organize each effect with the discovery of a cause, the end result is to blame some perception of misfortune on the experiencer.

Since the soul views everything as a gift of opportunity, vibration couldn't be the reason for why things occur. The Universe does not judge any of its creations or orchestrate reality from less than a perfect standpoint. In reality, vibration doesn't determine what does or doesn't happen to you. Instead, vibration determines your level of *resilience*: how quickly you pick yourself up from each unexpected crash and how gracefully you move through uncertainty with no one, including yourself, to be blamed for the change taking place.

While raising your vibration is a pivotal spiritual practice, it does nothing to stack the deck of outcome in your favor. Equally so, anyone without a practice of raising their vibration is equally as likely to manifest the outcomes of renewal and erosion that come to life in each of our journeys. The benefit of raising your vibration is having a useful amount of space between you and your external experiences, so that any emotions getting triggered as a result of your life circumstances invoke neither more shutting down nor lashing out at yourself or others. In the new spiritual paradigm, we raise our vibration to allow forgiveness and self-compassion to be more instinctive, just as we practice self-forgiveness and forgiveness as ways of raising our vibration even further.

Instead of racing against time, hoping to raise your vibration in an attempt to free yourself from the anticipation of more pain, just keep in mind: every being had to be a child before they could become an adult. Energetically speaking, every person has to start off at the lowest vibration in order to create a foundation that leads to the highest. Since neither the lowest nor highest vibration ensures all pleasure or only pain, we embrace vibrational alignment as how willing we are to either go with the flow or fight with life. When loving yourself through each unexpected loss or hardship replaces the need to dissect yourself under a spiritual microscope, or judge the actions of others, you will celebrate the resilience and awareness of high vibrational realities in their most practical embodied expressions.

From this space, you no longer judge abundance or misfortune on energy fields, as if vibration were a spiritual form of social status. Instead, you are here to cultivate great compassion for all the circumstances everyone has faced and are likely to encounter, simply as a means of inspiring highest truths into being. When you have done nothing wrong, the old-school notion of blaming anything on your experiences could only be a superstitious way of refusing the gifts the Universe planned to give you.

GOLDEN RULE #2

ANYONE WHO BLAMES YOU ISN'T HAPPY

It had been about five years since I came home to California to visit with friends, having removed myself from my old life to begin a new chapter of my career in Washington State. I didn't have to make many arrangements to see those I remember. Most encounters were brimming with a magical sense of nostalgia. It felt like I was watching a reunion episode of my favorite childhood TV show, seeing what had happened to those treasured characters I had come to know. Just visiting the same old locations while watching familiar faces pop up in my reality. Seeing how the friends I had known for so many years had grown up to become newer versions of themselves, just as I had when I decided to move away and plunge headfirst into my spiritual work.

Then I ran into a different type of friend—one who didn't know I was coming into town and felt left out for not knowing ahead of time. Her eyes pierced me with betrayal while attempting to mask it in passive-aggressive fashion.

"You've put on some weight," she said.

"Yes, I have," I replied, with such a depth of openness in recognition of how successfully I had added ten extra pounds to my five-foot-one stature.

I could sense the game playing out. This person sought to assert dominance on a subconscious level by pointing out something lacking in their view of me. By pointing out my physical appearance, she lessened the blow of self-imposed rejection.

Knowing I couldn't be the extent of her disdain, I asked her how she was doing.

With vague answers of "in transition" and "trying to sort things out," I knew that she was struggling to find her place in the world.

"I understand how you feel. I found my purpose and moved to Washington to pursue it without distraction. I'm sure the same inspiration will come your way," I said.

Her eyes welled up with equal parts desire for the inspiration I mentioned and regret for life choices she was still sorting out. She then said, "I've really missed you."

Out of respect from the opening that brought forth authenticity in place of sarcasm, projection, and passive-aggressive behavior, I smiled and said, "Thank you. It feels really nice to be missed."

With a puzzled look on her face, she asked, "You haven't missed me?"

I replied, "I'm not sure I miss anything in my life anymore. I see people when I see them, and until that happens, I do what I'm called to do."

She asked, "What's that like?"

I replied, "Happiness."

Our nearly existential dialogue got interrupted by the phone ringing. She had to take the call and wished me well. As I walked away, I was grateful for the opportunity to confirm the importance of my life choices, challenged only by those still searching for the happiness that had found me. I walked away in peace.

Just as I illustrated with the stories of my mom's anger in the previous chapter, the second Golden Rule reminds you: *"Anyone who blames you isn't happy."*

How many times in your life have you blamed yourself in a state of happiness? How many times have you blamed happily? It's nearly impossible, because those who blame are not happy. At our core, we are all such sensitive, heart-centered beings that the thought that anyone who blames us is unhappy can kind of feel like a form of blame unto itself. Such an acceptance is not actually a judgment—it's an awareness.

To see that someone who blames you, or a moment where you blame someone else, is because of one's relationship with happiness or unhappiness—is to see through the eyes of forgiveness.

Forgiveness is one of your highest attributes. It is the merciful grace of compassion in action. Forgiveness is not just accepting an apology; it is the willingness to respond to hurt by saying: "I'm sorry that *your unhappiness* has caused you to treat me this way."

True forgiveness is recognizing the relationship between people's most hurtful choices to their degree of unhappiness. On a soul level, if someone's ego is treating you unfairly, it's a way of saying, "I'm terribly unhappy, and my conduct is to show you how unhappy I am."

When someone's in their ego, they're not aware their attitude and behavior are associated with their degree of happiness. This is one of the main insights people are unaware of when operating from a state of unconsciousness. When people are unhappy, what's their viewpoint? I'm unhappy with *you*. In unconsciousness, you're the reason for someone's happiness or unhappiness. Being the reason for someone's happiness is a form of co-dependency and being the reason for some else's unhappiness is a projection of blame. Even if you blame yourself, it's just your soul's way of reminding you how unhappy you are. In every stage of your life's journey, there's the ego's viewpoint and the soul's perspective. The ego says, "I'm happy or unhappy because . . ." Meanwhile, the soul says, "You are only attached to outcomes being a certain way because of how unhappy you are." When you let go, you don't have to put yourself in toxic relationships as a measurement of self-acceptance. Equally so, when you're emotionally free, other peoples' experiences don't tend to affect you.

To allow this truth to be viscerally felt in your body, please repeat the following words, either silently or out loud:

Other people only affect me
to show me how unhappy I truly am.
When I'm happy,
people, places, and things
add to my happiness.
But nothing takes it away.
Because anyone who blames me
is only doing so
from a state of unhappiness.
And from that perception,

I offer forgiveness
by saying in my heart,
or if I can, out loud:
"I'm sorry your unhappiness
causes you to be this way."
Because most people who are unhappy
are not aware of their unhappiness;
they're too busy blaming.
So, from this moment forward,
I don't allow other people's blame
or unhappiness
to take away from the happiness
already within me.
Happiness is not something
I have to work hard to achieve.
It is simply the blame-free zone
of heart-centered consciousness.
And, if I'm blamed for my happiness,
it could only be from someone else's unhappiness,
as their ego's way of saying,
"I don't know how to find in myself
what you have found in you."

UNPACKING UNHAPPINESS

While it is common to walk around wondering what in the world will make you happy, it overlooks the more insightful realization of admitting that you don't know how to be happy. While we all know, on some level, that happiness comes from within, the confession of not knowing how to be happy simply helps you acknowledge that you rely on outside circumstances, characters, and outcomes as the *main source* of your fulfillment. The measurement of how much you rely on the outside world for your validation, sustenance, and approval is determined by how unhappy you already are. From this state of unhappiness, anyone, including yourself, may become the blame for why you feel so unfulfilled. Deeper than the surface of blame, there exists a depth of happiness where there is everything to acknowledge and nothing to blame.

Here's an easy way to remember this insight:

The moment you blame,
you've turned away
from the vibration of happiness.
So, what if you simply dared
to not blame those who choose to blame you?

Feel that for a moment. What if you didn't divide yourself from whatever degree of happiness you have in your life by blaming those who are blaming you? This is how we begin to break the cycle of abuse in our lives. It is how we assist the world in no longer requiring violence to be aware of the pain that so many are in need of processing.

The confusing part is seeing people in relative states of happiness, where they tend to blame only in the areas where they are not truly fulfilled. Those who are unhappy with their work life blame co-workers. Those who are unhappy at home blame their partners. Those who are unhappy with their past blame their family. Those who lack confidence blame their circumstances. Those who lack self-worth blame themselves.

No matter the projection or accusation, instead of blaming, forgiveness says, "I'm sorry that your unhappiness causes you to be this way with me. I'm sorry your unhappiness inspires you to steal some of *my* happiness, in an attempt to make it your own. I'm sorry that you see me as an object that you are attempting to use to enhance the object you've defined yourself to be. I cannot make you happy in any way. I can only help you remind yourself how unhappy you already are."

DOORWAYS TO GREATER HAPPINESS

Those who are happy are the most willing to forgive. Therefore, it is the cultivation of forgiveness that allows you to recognize, feel, and demonstrate the happiness that is always within you.

When you abide in the truth of forgiveness, you are saying from your soul to another, "What you did is not okay, *but I don't blame you.*" From the viewpoint of a loving Universe, people only act the way they do—blaming you, even mistreating you—to show you how unhappy they truly are. Since forgiveness is a cornerstone of happiness, the forgiveness you offer another helps energetically break cycles of abuse in both lives. As a result, it serves to usher in greater happiness for the forgiver and blessings of emotional healing for the person being forgiven.

Forgiveness is not a way of justifying cruel behavior. It is a way of refusing to store someone else's unhappiness in your cellular body as memories of mistreatment. Each time you forgive, the imprint someone's unconscious acts leaves in your body is cleared out and returned to their energy field as blessings of evolution. From this standpoint, the act of forgiving helps not only to free others from the unhappiness causing them to withdraw, shut down, or lash out but also to free you from walking this earth as anyone's victim. From this depth of understanding, forgiveness is not passive submission but an active form of liberation in action.

From the standpoint of forgiveness, conflict is when two people say to each other, "Here's how I need you to be." Resolution is when one of those two people says, "I may not be able to give you what you want, and you certainly may not be the one for me, but I don't blame you for your unhappiness. I allow you to be exactly as you are."

YOUR MANTRA FOR RULE #2

To cultivate the attribute of forgiveness, please read silently or repeat out loud the following words:

I allow
those who blame and have wronged me
to be forgiven.
In forgiving others, I am set free.

When you are embodying your soul, you are seeing and living life as divinity in physical form. When you are living in the ego's perspective, you are divinity in its potential, but living in some degree of separation from your own divine nature. Imagine this from a cosmic level. When you say, "I allow those who have blamed and wronged me to be forgiven," you're actually speaking from your highest God nature. You are deciding someone's forgiveness by allowing the Universe to carry it out. You just have to *permit* forgiveness. The people who need forgiveness the most are the people who treat you the worst, because they're the most entrenched in their egos, needing the relief of forgiveness to inspire the awakening of their soul, to spare more people from being mistreated.

Once you start to align with the true essence of forgiveness, you no longer require the world to show you its unhappiness by overlooking or mistreating you.

As you will come to see, when you become aware of how unhappy so many people are, you cultivate *more* happiness for all by being more forgiving. As forgiveness becomes an instinct, you are less likely to blame others, even those who subconsciously beg for emotional healing by lashing out at you.

EXERCISE: Assisting in the Healing of Others

Make a list of those in your life who have blamed you or those in the world suffering far worse than you. One by one, send blessings of forgiveness to each person. How much better do you feel when focusing on assisting in the healing of others?

SPIRITUAL MYTH-BUSTING: "The outside world reflects my inner state of being."

When you embrace the wisdom of Golden Rule #2, you help dispel old-paradigm myths that suggest the outside world is always a reflection of your inner reality. I have experienced countless spiritual beings who misunderstand this teaching, and it always comes off as a form of spiritual co-dependency. As if the mean-spirited behavior of another unhappy person reflects any meanness or unhappiness within you. While human beings gain insight by organizing chaos with relationships between effects and their perceived causes, it is such an oversimplification and subtle act of self-abuse to blame the experiencer for the actions of others.

From an individual standpoint, the outside world could never reflect your inner reality, since Golden Rule #1 reminds you: "You've done nothing wrong." Furthermore, Golden Rule #2 tells you: "Those who blame you are unhappy." It's not wrong for others to be unhappy, and it's not wrong in the eyes of the Universe for others to remind you of their unhappiness, if the Universe allowed it to be. If it happens, there are insights to glean and gifts to receive for the evolution of both journeys.

As I stated in my second book, *Everything Is Here to Help You,* those who are mean or acting out of anger are begging for space to integrate the healing they most likely don't know is underway. When others mistreat us, both souls are playing out a scenario of expansion, which blesses the forgiver and the one being forgiven with the inevitable gifts of greater alignment and expanded awareness.

When believing the outside reflects the inside, you are defining *yourself* as the problem. When the outside merely shows you who needs more space versus more of your presence, you are not the problem but the very solution being birthed in both hearts. In reality, life *is* a mirror, but the question is, what's being reflected? When life is a mirror, the light within you is honored as the creations of form around you. And yet, even though each person is an extension of your divinity, on a relative human level, each person has their own journey from ego to soul. Therefore, the actions of other egos reflect or suggest nothing about your ego, unless you take responsibility for other people's behavior as expressions of co-dependency.

Because divinity is the truth of all, the only reality the mirror of life could reflect is the light of your soul's essence. The more forgiving you become, the happier you'll be. The happier you are, the more aligned you are with your soul. The more aligned with your soul, the more you see reflections of your own light in others, since the brightness of your divinity could only bring forward the brightness of those around you. That is the interconnected magic of unity consciousness.

Everything tends to grow upward or move forward, never to go backward in evolution. Flowers begin as seeds but never go back once in bloom. In the same way, the ego dissolves as the soul emerges. Your emerging light can become so potent within your being that you begin observing the innocent beauty of all as reflections of your awakening soul.

GOLDEN RULE #3

HARDSHIPS CAN BE FAST-TRACKED THROUGH THANKFULNESS

I've always been singled out by others for being different. Most of the time, this seemed to attract bullying from other kids who were looking for someone to suppress and dominate.

I never cracked this code in childhood. I just endured each verbal jab, and on a few occasions, physical pain, from those who gained amusement from the misfortune of others. This helped further establish my co-dependent tendencies, since now, upsetting others wasn't just the loss of validation but another potential moment of harassment. As I grew up, abuse from bullies faded away and transformed into verbal pokes from distant relatives I'd see at various gatherings and reunions. By this time, I was mostly free of my people-pleasing tendencies, having developed the thick skin needed to stop blaming my behavior for someone else's judgment. Somewhere along the way, during a moment of sarcastic banter with a relative, I received an intuition in the form of a question, *What if you said thank you in response to any insult, judgment, or projection?*

Such an idea seemed strangely out of place, in response to an insult versus a compliment, but that's what intrigued me the most. *What if I didn't respond to their criticism, but received it from the consciousness of my intention?* I thought. At that moment something deep inside me clicked into place. Since my daily intention had been and continues to be, "May I be a gift that is received in the lives of everyone I encounter," what if I received even an insult as a gift sent from their divinity, even if gift wrapped by the projections of their ego?

It was such a ridiculously liberating suggestion that I had to test it out. Later that night, I crossed paths with one of the relatives I mentioned earlier.

His once-subtle forms of judgment had now become a boisterous alcohol-fueled witch hunt. With slurred words, he looked at me and said, "You know what your problem is?"

Truly without an awareness of what problem he was referring to, I responded, "No, I don't, but I'd love to hear what you have to say."

"Your problem is—you're just weird. I mean, who makes a living as a healer?"

The others watching from their chairs and couches gasped. I looked directly into his eyes, smiled, and said, "There are many people in need of healing. Perhaps you're not one of them. Thank you." The last part is what their ego latched on to since it was so out of context to the insult offered.

"What are you thanking me for?" he asked.

"Thank you for your feedback. I'm always interested in what you have to say."

Then there was a pause. His drunken rant was momentarily interrupted when I spoke to the innocence he had lost touch with many years ago. As a way of saving face and denying the vulnerable invitation I offered, he said, "I just don't know why you'd thank me."

To which I replied, perfectly on cue, "What can I say? I'm weird."

The entire room laughed while my drunken relative slumped away into the farthest corner of the house to further bury his unprocessed pain with more booze.

It was at that defining moment of conscious interaction where any threat of confrontation inspired me to recognize the person's soul as a gift to receive instead of responding to the unconsciousness they weren't prepared to take responsibility for or even acknowledge. As I continued this practice, in response to compliments as well as judgments, my willingness to say *thank you* became one of the most popular phrases I found myself saying countless times a day. As I became aligned in the vibration of gratitude, I began to notice how the pattern of bullying or confrontation had disappeared from my life. I began to see that my constant and authentic usage of the words *thank you* shifted my field of reality to bring me only outcomes, interactions, and characters whose contribution in my life matched the gratitude I constantly sent out. It wasn't as if I planned to say *thank you* hundreds of times a day as a way of eliminating any mistreatment. It never occurred to me, since the Universe doesn't respond to actions expressed from a space of manipulation or coercion.

Instead, I just came to see how good it felt to receive everything as a gift, allowing any judgment of ego to be a moment of playing peek-a-boo with someone else's soul. I also found the practice of thankfulness to be a way of sending blessings of forgiveness in advance. Instead of waiting for someone's ego to wrong me as a reminder of who needed the healing effects of forgiveness, I lead with *thank you* as a way of giving them the transformative effects of gratitude. As *thank you* became hardwired into me, the little boy who spent the majority of his life hiding from moments of judgment, denial, exclusion, embarrassment, and ridicule felt safe enough to step forward and merge with my adult self. This gave me the ability to open my heart to a greater capacity without being a larger moving target for other people's insecurities and frustrations.

This highlights the third Golden Rule: "*Hardships can be fast-tracked through moments of thankfulness.*" Hardship is how your nervous system responds to adversity. Adversity is how you perceive and relate to change or loss. Change and loss are some of the deepest ways in which life evolves you out of ego and into alignment with your soul. Change and loss occur through moments of renewal and erosion that come and go like the seasons or weather patterns. As you experience the nature of change and loss from the soul's sense of excitement, instead of the ego's perception of judgment, you are able to let go with authenticity and ease. Only the soul lets go. Equally so, all the ego can do is maintain struggle, judgment, and negotiation. With the utmost respect for its purpose in your evolution, what's the battle cry of ego—"I wasn't ready to let go of that yet." The ego will never be ready to let go of *anything. It can't* because to let go is to accept evolution. You may wonder, "Why can't the ego accept evolution?" Because evolution requires leaving the ego behind; therefore, the ego cannot agree to something it cannot be a part of.

With enough time and experience steeping in heart-centered consciousness, the ego releases its control as a result of your alignment with thankfulness.

YOUR MANTRA FOR RULE #3

Whether silently or out loud, repeat the following words:

Thank you for this gift.

Notice the way the sentence is constructed. It begins with *thank you,* which is anchoring the vibration of gratitude, or thankfulness. The sentence ends with *gift,* which is the affirmation that something is only here to positively move you forward in evolution—no matter the circumstances in view. It's literally a cosmic rule that anything received as a gift will always contain some form of benefit. When not viewed as a gift coming your way, such a creation is given permission to be anything else but helpful within your reality.

To further demonstrate the potency of thanking everything as a gift, I have personally tested the boundaries of *thank you* by acknowledging the gift in all levels of human experience. I remember one specific instance of exploring it. While sitting in meditation, I spontaneously had the idea of thinking about the worst things that have ever happened to me. One by one, I called upon each character who hurt, wronged, shamed, abused, or betrayed me, and I said to them, "Thank you for this gift." From the insignificant moments of annoyance to the deepest pains I've ever felt, I thanked each person who has been a part of my life with a sincere depth of gratefulness for their contribution. I did this from the knowing that if even one single detail about my past were to be altered, I would never have become exactly who I am today. Therefore, my gratefulness came from a place of pure self-acceptance, which created absolutely no space for anger, frustration, regret, or vengeance to lurk. In being thankful for every moment that made me the man I'm so proud to be, "Thank you for this gift" became the words to celebrate the confirmation that forgiveness was complete.

In essence, you forgive others to help them become more forgiving. In forgiveness, you unearth the energy of happiness, which makes thankfulness more instinctive. As you cultivate greater happiness and thankfulness by being more forgiving, the true self-acceptance of your soul's reality awakens. Once you are proud to be the person every single moment in time helped you become, there is only gratitude to be offered, helping to energetically break the cycles of abuse in others and unravel patterns of violence permeating our planet, so that each and every sentient being can be nourished by the validation that only we can give ourselves. And so true freedom is here.

EXERCISE: Cultivating the Opposite

Think of a person in your life who either hurt you the most or is the hardest to forgive.

Find the adjective that describes the way they made you feel. Was it betrayed, ashamed, hurt, heartbroken, devastated, or another word that best describes the intensity of your experience?

Here is the crucial turning point. What is the *opposite* adjective to how they made you feel? If it was abandonment, the opposite of abandonment is inclusion. Because abandonment is to be cast away by another. Inclusion is to be accepted by another.

If it was heartbreak, the opposite of heartbreak is wholeness. If it was devastation, the opposite of devastation is openness. If it was pain, the opposite of pain is ease. If it was shame, the opposite of shame is worthiness. If it was betrayal, the opposite of betrayal is trust.

Why am I showing you this? Because every negative experience that someone seemed to bring upon you serves to help you cultivate the opposite adjective on a vibrational level.

Through devastation, we eventually arrive at more openness. Through betrayal, we actually learn to trust ourselves deeper. Through heartbreak, we become more open. Through abuse, we become more compassionate.

No one deserves anything that happens to them. Life is not a matter of deserving. It's an opportunity. A divine rite of passage.

Through this practice, you take the worst thing that happened to you, the adjective that describes the way that it made you feel, and acknowledge that the opposite of this feeling is what you're *actually* being given the chance to cultivate throughout your life's journey.

Can you now visualize the person who wronged you and try speaking these words out loud:

Thank you for this gift.
I may not have liked the gift
when I initially opened the package.
But there is no doubt
it's only destined to make me
better than I've ever been before.
This doesn't make the action okay.
And the fact that it isn't okay
is why I offer forgiveness.
To ensure no one else may be harmed
by the actions of unprocessed pain.
If there's any justice in this world,
may I be more evolved
than those who have hurt me.
So, in knowing my deepest pain,
I guarantee that no one in my presence
shall ever endure the pain
that I have endured.
This helps me break the cycle of abuse.
Through forgiveness, unfairness is a gift
that only helps me be more kind.
Thank you, unfairness.
Thank you for this gift.

If there's something in your life that doesn't feel like a gift, just sit with this wisdom until it feels authentic. It's not a gift *until* it's a gift. You might need to start with "thank you for this hardship, thank you for this betrayal, thank you for this abuse, thank you." If you can at least say *thank you* to some of the worst things that have ever happened to you, on a vibrational level, you will feel something deep inside of you shift. When it occurs, it is always the presence of forgiveness answering your call to make things right.

A HEAVENLY PERSPECTIVE

When I was eight years old, I left my body and visited heaven. Since then, I've had an open dialogue with the Universe. Of all the insights I've learned throughout my life, I've learned by seeing firsthand, there is an afterlife. When you're in heaven, there are questions that are asked of you. I'll share with you one of the lesser-known questions you're asked in heaven. It's a question of extraordinary perspective. There's the question of how deeply you loved, of your regrets, but here's a rather clear and definitive question:

How many people did you hurt as a result of the hurt you endured?

I'm sure you've heard the phrase, "Hurt people hurt people." I like to say, "Free people free people." You might ask, "What does it mean to be free?" Being free means you might get hurt, but you will not hurt others as an excuse for being hurt. Being free means you are here to break cycles of abuse by saying *thank you* to any perceivable hurt. Only the soul can do this. If any degree of ego hears these words, it is immediately frightened or repelled.

As always, you can work the three-step process outlined in this chapter:

1. How do I feel as a result of this hurt?
2. What's the opposite adjective?
3. Thank you for helping me cultivate this quality of my soul's potential.

One of the most compelling reasons why the image of Christ on a cross is a vivid depiction of surrender is because the one being crucified isn't fighting back. How many beings did Christ hurt as a result of his hurt? Zero. That's the path of mastery. You might be hurt throughout your life, but your objective is to hurt no one in response. Your ego might think, "If I don't hurt the people who hurt me, what do I do?" To which the soul replies, "Say thank you." If you're entrenched in ego, that will make no sense at all. It will sound completely insane. If, however, you're an evolving soul, something in you says, "You know, that makes sense, somehow."

It's actually the only way. Once you are ready, willing, and able to bring gratitude to the forefront, you'll be surprised how often people go out of their way to help, uplift, and support you. Simply put, the light within every being steps forward once the divinity in you shows up.

This means the speed at which you evolve is how often you bring gratitude to the table. When everything is a gift, you have successfully completed Golden Rule #3.

SPIRITUAL MYTH-BUSTING: "Reality grows where attention goes."

When you embrace the wisdom of Golden Rule #3, you help to dispel old-paradigm myths such as the age-old saying, "Reality grows where attention goes." This is not a true statement at all. If anything, it is one of the most fear-based ideas that gave rise to the positive thinking movement of the 70s and 80s. In retrospect, it did more to create spiritual ego's fear of negativity than it aligned human beings with the light of divinity.

Let's first acknowledge the sliver of truth this statement is suggesting. If you choose to see things from a negative viewpoint on a regular basis, through the law of repetition, you increase the likelihood that your subconscious mind will be fed by such perspectives. As a result, you will seek out negativity to confirm what you've conditioned yourself to believe. This might be a groundbreaking realization for narcissistic behavior, but for the already evolving, energetically sensitive soul, it just creates more superstitious belief patterns to be afraid of.

Can you multiply your debt just by staring at your credit card bill? No. Why? Because reality doesn't grow where attention goes. If you were to believe such an oversimplified statement, you would be more than likely to turn away from someone in pain, out of the fear of manifesting equal amounts of adversity if you focus too much on it. Especially knowing, our role as lightworkers, earth angels, and evolving spiritual masters invites you to thank each and every person for the gifts they provide, whether good or bad, as our way of elevating our vibration through the power of gratitude and forgiveness. You can't participate in that depth of global and individual transformation if you believe these types of antiquated statements.

It all comes down to human beings not having the coping skills to be aware of why adversity strikes and how to use each moment toward the evolutionary advantage of all. As a whole, we are so afraid of attracting more difficulty and upsetting the never-satisfied ego structure that we are more willing to turn away from the hardships of another if it guarantees us one split second of joy. Thankfully, we have arrived at a pivotal time in Earth's evolution, where the pain of humanity is so severe and relentless, it forces us to ask the deeper questions as entry points into a more mature, spiritually aligned reality.

Gone are the days when supposedly positive people disempower the hardships of other people's testimony, as if the feedback they provide about the depth of their difficulties is somehow lowering anyone's vibration. Of all the mechanisms that restrict the flow of consciousness and maintain a lower vibration, there is no greater culprit than denial. When you feel sad, low, or exhausted by other people's feedback, it's because you are empathizing with their experience. If you wish to transform such exhaustion into lightness, inspiration, and joy, simply respond with spoken blessings for a better tomorrow. You don't even have to take the time to convince anyone how everything is a gift. That's for you to know on the inside, while leading with your most loving responses toward those who may not have even taken a moment to breathe since the last catastrophe struck.

Life is a dance of ever-growing perspective that cannot be disrespected with oversimplification. Let us join together, daring to look at life's most insurmountable difficulties directly, while asking the most important question only your soul can muster, "How can I help?"

Through the power of thankfulness that fast-tracks adversities into the soul's domain of infinite excitement, I invite you to embrace Golden Rule #3. One moment of gratitude at a time, it eradicates any tendency to be less emotionally available for those who just need to know they are seen, heard, and loved.

GOLDEN RULE #4

FEELING BETTER HELPS EVERYONE HEAL

I've always had an incredibly intimate relationship with death. For many, death feels like the ultimate mystery, where everything you know and love is snuffed away whenever anyone's time has come. In my experience, death has never been a thief, but a *doorway* into liberation for those who dare to leap without the need to look. Not from book knowledge or anything else but the razor-sharp instincts of my intuitive guidance, death has always felt like a friend.

From this kinship with death, I've often been called into moments of existential crisis, as members of my family stood between worlds. Whether it was my grandmother, my dad, or even my mom, I have helped each of my closest family members cross over into the afterlife due to an inexplicable ability to be calm, centered, and open at the peak of emotional intensity.

I remember being at their bedsides, surrounded by family members who were already processing the loss of the loved one that hadn't yet let go. I say this with absolutely no judgment for their experience. If anything, I've judged my own experience, thinking that expressing a lack of sadness or disarray must mean I am far less caring of a person. While many of my family members played out the conditioning of not being able to be open in time of loss, I always entered the scene grounded, joyful, and happy to see everyone—including those about to pass. This wasn't a planned-out approach, but just how openly I meet moments of uncertainty. When life becomes a big question mark, I literally feel the wheel of time stop. While this might frighten the ego structures of most people, it actually brings me profound amounts of peace. This is because the energy that enters to escort a soul back home to the light is the level of consciousness I have embodied for many years. It's called samadhi, or a state of uninterrupted living meditation. For some people, samadhi can only be accessed in the afterlife. As awakening beings, we are able to access and embody the consciousness of life after death without having to die in order to live freely.

I remember people looking at me as I greeted my dying loved ones with joyful smiles. They may have been heavily medicated, or deranged, but the fits of torment and waves of pain they felt before I arrived subsided soon after I entered the room. I don't think of this as a special power I bestow, but the rightful privilege to be a vessel for the light to do its best work. Less than an hour after I arrive with smiles to soothe the hearts of all, my family member takes their final breath, leaving this world for the next chapter of existence that welcomes them in.

I've often been asked by my relatives, "How do you do that?" My answer is simple. I feel so good about where each person is going that it soothes their nervous system into peacefully letting go. Having visited heaven when I was eight, I know firsthand the transcendent glory awaiting every heart at the end of their journey. I feel it is my duty to do all that I can to bridge both worlds energetically, to allow the end of one lifetime to simply be a doorway into the next highest level. Looking back, this is how Golden Rule #4 was introduced to me.

The fourth Golden Rule says, *"Feeling better helps everyone heal."* As energetically sensitive beings, we tend to develop co-dependent relationships mainly due to worrying that our light will be too bright for other people. We often feel bad about our happiness because of the unhappiness other people may have in *their* lives. Because we don't want anyone to feel left out, we wind up lowering our vibration so that other people have companionship. Then we have to work as quickly as possible to help other people heal as a way of returning to the happiness we've abandoned in ourselves. From a personal perspective, this was the exact pattern I played out for the majority of my life. When you are energetically sensitive, you are known as an empath. An empath means you often match and mirror the emotions of others. Why does this occur? What creates this empathic tendency to abandon your happiness and become just as displaced and unhappy as those around you?

To understand this, we look at the play of energy. Whoever is having the more intense sensation or is more committed to their experience, is the one who wins the energetic game. The one who's more entrenched or committed to their emotional experience dominates the experience emotionally. The person who's not as committed winds up matching the other person's experience. This can go one of two different ways: It means that if you are around someone who's more committed to their victimhood than you are to your light, then you'll wind up feeling *their* victimhood as your own. Equally so, if you are more committed to the light than someone is to identifying with their pain, you can radiate a frequency of light that invites their subconscious mind to match the vibration you're transmitting. You can be a mirror that reflects the light of their soul and unravels the attachments of their ego, depending on how committed you are to the light within you. All too often, the light realms can feel like passive states, while the shadow realms feel more aggressive in nature. When a very loving but gentle person stands in the presence of an aggressively reactive person, because their shadow is more intense than often your light is illuminated, you are likely to lower your vibration to match them as a companion in their pain. That's why we empath. To innocently ensure that no one suffers alone or feels excluded, only to lower the vibration of light we were born to shine.

Don't dim your light in any way. Shining less helps no one transform. Let's say you're in the presence of someone who's unhappy. Maybe for this person, there's a benefit of being in the presence of your light, but they could only bask in your brightness for a few minutes before needing to integrate all the light you shine. At that time, they will either become upset, push you away, storm off, or find an excuse to go somewhere else. If you're in your ego, you're likely to take it as a moment of rejection. If, however, you're rooted in your soul, you will acknowledge it as a confirmation of what is best for this person's journey. There is a specific amount of time anyone is meant to be in the presence of another. When the time has come to integrate all the gifts they have received, they may seem suddenly avoidant. If they are exposed to the light of another longer than need be, anger may arise. This helps the modern-day empath view the ego's perception of rejection as the soul's awareness of redirection—always being guided to where one needs to be for their evolution.

SHINING YOUR RADIANT LIGHT

Everyone wants to be warmed by the light of the sun. But if you stay too long, the light that warms you starts to dissolve the things getting warmed. Metaphorically speaking, to be dissolved by the heat of the sun is only to merge into and become the thing that was warming you.

When shifting from ego to soul, you are becoming one with the light within yourself. One of the first steps of becoming that light is allowing yourself to shine at full capacity—no matter the circumstances in view. It's not that people can't deal with your perfection, it's that people don't know how to deal with their *own* perfection. An ego would rather see itself as imperfect because at least it's understandable. That which is understandable gives the ego something to manage and maintain. There is no role in perfection. There is nothing for the ego to do. This is why it settles for lesser, more understandable versions of self.

In order for you to shine your light, without first needing every ego in your life to sign a waiver releasing you of any liability that your light is going to bring into their reality, it is essential to develop the soul's attribute of trust. Trusting that what you bring forth within you, as the light of divinity for yourself, for your family, and for your world, is going to help each person you meet. It may or may not be immediate, but it will always be the very gift each person needs to complete each stage of their journey. This is why it requires trust for you to shine your light into this world. A world that is meant to be healed by a depth of goodness most people can't receive unless they work hard enough to receive it. In truth, no hard work is required. Just a steadfast willingness to remain open, even when every heart around you has found ample proof to justify shutting down.

YOUR MANTRA FOR RULE #4

Whether read silently or spoken aloud, the mantra that helps you cultivate the soul's attribute of trust is:

My happiness is a service to all.

Your happiness is not the end result of shuffling the furniture of your life in a more preferable way. The secret is learning to enjoy being around people, even when they don't enjoy being around themselves. In recalling the wisdom of Golden Rule #2, those who blame you are unhappy. Therefore, someone who is mean, nasty, and unhappy doesn't like being who they are. The unfortunate thing is, people who don't like being who they are often make it not so easy for other people to be around them. That's the deepest truth of the statement "misery loves company." Our job, our mission, as empaths, is daring in the most authentic way to creatively find ways to enjoy being around those who don't enjoy being around themselves. From this space, the light you shine, no matter how others respond, helps to free others from the patterning of their most ingrained reactions.

EXERCISE: Daring to Admire

Can you dare to *admire* the people who are difficult for you to be around? What can you authentically admire about them? Even if it begins with, "I admire the qualities they are helping me cultivate by being around such a difficult person."

What is this person helping you cultivate? Greater patience? Deeper forgiveness? Is their closed mindedness or emotional rigidity allowing you a chance to be more open-minded and heart-centered?

What happens in your experience when you dare to admire the people who are the hardest for you to be around?

ANGELS IN TRAINING

When you're a conscious being, anything you encounter has been created to make you *more* conscious. If you're an unconscious being, anything you encounter is likely to create more unconscious responses—that is, until you're ready to wake up. When consciousness awakens, it only becomes more awake and conscious. As an empath, you're already on that trajectory. Prior to birth, you've already surrendered, which is what gave you the strength to incarnate and be as you are. Since you're already waking up, all life can do is wake you up further. In order to do so, all life has to decide is what combination of characters, outcomes, situations, and circumstances you require in order for your light to shine at full capacity. In every breath, that's what life is doing.

When you embrace the wisdom of Golden Rule #4, you cultivate the attribute of trust. If you trust that your happiness is a service to others, your well-being will be an agent of change—a catalyst of growth that helps everyone heal. Feeling bad for other people feeling bad doesn't help anyone feel better. But, daring to feel good about the uniqueness and innocence of others helps those who feel bad to accelerate their healing.

SPIRITUAL MYTH-BUSTING: "You must dissolve darkness in order to shine your light."

Each of us incarnates with a specific amount of density to dissolve, while also having a vast array of light to shine. In an oversimplified spiritual approach, you have been led to believe you must first cleanse yourself of darkness before your light has permission to shine. Nothing could be further from the truth. The arising of light occurs through inspired moments of selfless action. Meanwhile, the density of shadow you are likely to transmute throughout this lifetime occurs through the reactivity of emotional response. In truth, the more often you act from a selfless space, the less reactivity arises from the actions of others.

It is not the countless hours you put into dissolving darkness that creates space for your light to shine. Instead, it is how open and receptive you are to serving a will beyond the threshold of individual gain that allows a transcendent light within you to come to life for the well-being of all. Working around the clock to clear your darkness, as if it's a prerequisite to shining your light, is only the approach when thinking of spiritual evolution from the *conditioned* belief of an education system. Needing enough credits in order to advance in grade may be the proper structure for evolving egos, but when it comes to the evolution of your *soul*, it is merely the amount of well-being that you pass along to others that determines the trajectory of your advancement. Since every reaction could only be the next gift to receive, it is your willingness to feel good about the contributions made on behalf of all that allows your happiness to serve the expansion of the whole.

The kingdom of heaven welcomes every being into the light, no matter the trials or tribulations that define their struggles. If heaven maintains such an open-door policy, why are you working so hard to be who you are? Perhaps there is a deeper truth that begs to be explored. Maybe it is only known the moment you let go.

GOLDEN RULE #5

WELL-BEING IS A SIGNAL THAT YOU ARE READY TO EMBODY YOUR POTENTIAL

Whether it was the love-hate relationship with kids on the playground, not knowing where I stood with my parents depending on their mood or stress level, or how people I knew responded to my desire to dive into my spiritual journey, I have always had an awareness of an invisible force carrying and guiding me along, no matter the roles anyone outside of me seemed to play. I wouldn't have put these pieces together until I was an adult, but looking back, I was always aware of the existence of well-being within me. For some reason, it never caused me to assume anything outside of me would make me feel well or even better. Instead, I was just as attached to personal outcome as anyone else, but instead of remaining attached to the hope of greater pleasure, I was hoping to avoid more pain.

This inherent awareness of well-being also created a rather unique entry point into following the impulse of my spiritual aspirations. Strangely, I wasn't on a spiritual path to discover well-being or chase away my pain. The indisputable calling of inner exploration was answered by one burning lifelong desire—to know and be one with God. From my earliest Sunday school learnings, I immediately felt a gravitational pull in this direction, much like a calling received to enter a seminary.

I remember sitting in Sunday school, listening to interpretations of what God is, while thinking: "That's not it at all." It felt more like a mystical Santa Claus sitting on a cloud, watching to determine which list your name goes on. As a child, I found this uninspired and almost silly, while captivated by a deeper inner yearning to know the deepest truth.

I remember the day that yearning for truth would be satisfied. I was in fifth grade at the time. It was one of those special school days in December where the afternoon was spent at a school assembly listening to the choir sing holiday songs. All of a sudden, I heard the most breathtakingly holy song I had ever heard: "Do you hear what I hear?" It literally felt like the ceiling had opened up with heaven's kingdom inviting me home. I literally was seconds away from a volcanic level emotional outburst. I had never in my life felt that emotionally moved and inspired—outside of my out of body experience I had a few year's prior. I remember thinking, "Everyone will look at me and laugh if I let this feeling out." With all my might, I stuffed this feeling down and moved as quickly as I could to go outside. As I made my way out of the auditorium, tears streamed down my face, just not with the initial intensity that wanted to be expressed. I wasn't sure why I was crying, but I wasn't hurt or in pain. Just coming unglued by the celestial hymns of a holiday song. After a few moments, it all settled down as I returned to the holiday assembly.

At the time I didn't know what it meant, but I knew something big had occurred. Looking back, it was the inherent well-being of my true nature beginning to awaken within me. A process that would ramp up in adulthood, where the well-being of Universal Truth would buff out each hiding spot of fear and reconstruct everything within me, so nothing but this heavenly potential would remain. My deepest desire was to know and be one with the will of God. In fifth grade on that fateful day, I was auspiciously informed that my prayer had been received.

No matter the reason you've been called inward to uncover your unique place in the Universe, it is the regular discovery of well-being that awakens life's highest potential, no matter the circumstances or stresses that fill your life. This is why the fifth Golden Rule reminds you: *"Well-being is a signal that you are ready to embody your potential."* The more often you recognize the presence of well-being within you, you are saying to the Universe, "I am aware of what is already right, perfect, and whole inside of me." If we can become aware of what is right, perfect, and whole inside of us, we begin to see what is right, perfect, and whole in the *Universe,* even throughout a human play of gain, loss, erosion, and renewal.

No matter the evidence in sight, you are already perfect, whole, and complete because the well-being you are free to notice acts as your proof. When you affirm that perfection and well-being is within you, it tells the Universe that you have the worthiness and emotional availability to receive more blessings in your life.

Well-being is the spray of the waterfall, and the waterfall is a cascading fountain of light or Source

Energy. When you get close to the Divine fountain of light, well-being is what soaks you. There is another name for this fountain of light that might be more recognizable. It exists as living proof that well-being and perfection are always alive and active inside you. It is none other than the very breath you breathe.

THE POWER OF BREATH

As you breathe in, you are taking in the light of existence, cleansing, purifying, and nourishing all aspects of your being. With each out-breath, all the light you've taken in goes out into the world for the healing, awakening, and well-being of every heart.

Whether you're aware of it or not, you're always breathing this light in and out. The question is, why don't you always feel the well-being if that's what well-being is? It is because your breath is only giving you the experience of your awareness of what breath is. If you think breath is just the very thing that keeps you alive, then that becomes the extent of your breathing experience. The more you become aware of what the breath actually is, as the living evidence of light within you, the more every single breath provides you with the well-being that becomes the contribution of expansion the world is destined to receive.

When you are aware of your breath as the infinite light of Source energy, every breath is given permission to heal your being. When you are aware of the breath at that level, you are more aligned with it on a regular basis. When you're more aligned with your breath, your thoughts become manifestations of aligned breathing, creating viewpoints, perceptions, and inspired ideas as harmonious, clear, and positive as the light you breathe. When you are aligned with breath, the words you speak become the gifts—no matter how unconscious anyone seems to be. The actions you choose, whether from a depth of nobility or a reaction of fear, are simply determined by how aligned your breathing has become. Of course, what creates alignment with your breath is knowing what the breath is. As you are beginning to see, the breath is the living evidence of well-being. It is the one eternal reality, flowing like a cascading fountain of eternal light. It is the very seed of Source energy. It is the remembrance of heaven's kingdom. It is your true self, as you've been and shall always be.

In order to embody the wisdom of Golden Rule #5, take as many moments as you need to align with your breath to allow the greater miracles of life to unfold on your behalf. No matter what kind of life you lead, if you want to improve the possibilities of your reality—deepen your relationship with breath.

You are a co-creator of reality. It is co-created by the power of your breath. The more aligned you are with breath, the better and the safer the world is to inhabit. When your breath is the very evidence of well-being, you are cultivating the attribute of focus.

Without focus, life lacks the depth and meaning that reveals the connectedness of love existing at the heart of every experience. When focused, you are able to develop harmonious relationships with others. With great focus, the left and right hemispheres of your brain work interdependently, instead of colliding in a battle of independence. From this space, the inner relationships between body and mind allow the heart to remain naturally open as the soul takes the place of the integrating ego. Since the deepening of inner and outer relationships occurs through the cultivation of focus, such focus can be developed along a heart-centered path when focusing on the two most important factors of the new spiritual paradigm.

The two most important factors are self-love and alignment with breath. In the new spiritual paradigm, you love yourself enough to be worthy of receiving your breath, while becoming one with your breath to deepen your worthiness to give and receive love. When these two factors are in focus, your inner and outer relationships blossom from the harmony of well-being, which signals to the Universe that you are ready to embody more of your infinite potential.

YOUR MANTRA FOR RULE #5

Please read silently or repeat out loud the following words:

My breath is the living presence of well-being. The more mindfully I breathe, the more alive I feel.

EXERCISE: Anchoring to Your Breath

To further anchor the wisdom of this mantra, please read the following words either silently or repeated out loud:

My mind is a manifestation of breath.
The more aligned with breath I am,
the clearer my mind becomes.

My body is a manifestation of breath.
The more aligned with breath I am,
the more vibrant and open my body becomes.

My emotions are a manifestation of breath.
The more aligned with breath I am,
the more harmonious my emotions shall be.

My world is a manifestation of breath.
The more aligned with breath I am,
the more fulfilling my relationships shall be.

Every aspect of reality
is a manifestation of breath.
The more aligned with breath I am,
the more real I shall be.

Instead of living
in the reality of my ego's fantasy
I shall dwell in the reality of my soul's eternal light,
where I can simply abide with my breath
as an announcer of well-being,
becoming aware that within me as my breath,
well-being and perfection are always existing.

And to signal to the Universe
that in recognizing my breath
as evidence of perfection
I am ready, willing, and able
to receive more perfection.

And to receive it with worthiness and joy
as a gift for myself
and for those
who don't know the worthiness
of their own eternal light,
allowing my happiness
to be a service to all.
And so I'm free.

SPIRITUAL MYTH-BUSTING: "You will be the most fulfilled around people of like mind."

There is a recurring fantasy throughout the spiritual journey. It stems from human beings' fascination with the ever-expanding nature of reality, and it remains natural and instinctive to want to process your discoveries with others to ensure you're not alone in the way life is seen. Sadly, if you're not with a partner who resonates or isn't acclimated to such perspectives, you are likely to pull away from the one who may be the most grounding and supportive person to help you integrate your most miraculous findings.

I have personally seen many seekers throw their old lives away in pursuit of groups or communities of like-minded individuals. With people of like mind, you are spared no relief from the same relationship patterns of a non-spiritual world. The same jealousies, lies, deception, projections, judgments, and hurt are spun, this time with spiritual ideologies as justification for unconscious behavior.

The need to be around like-minded people is how cults get created. The avoidance of cult activity occurs in communities of independent thinkers, who respect the uniqueness and contributions of others for the joint purpose of collective harmony. The notion that the grass is greener on the spiritual side of reality is only a belief one holds to be true prior to exploring the truth for themselves. Upon such an exploration, you will find that whether someone wears a religious robe, a pageant crown, or spends all their time meditating, the patterns of ego and expressions of the soul are equally present and uniquely expressed for every person. The belief that a group of people saying the same things, doing the same practices, and living the same way is better remains a dream to chase when the current terms and conditions of your reality give your ego no room to breathe.

Using the wisdom of Golden Rule #5, your desire to be around those who embody their highest potential is not something to pursue, but a reality to attract by noticing the presence of well-being *within* you. As this occurs by spending more time with your breath, you are able to call forward members of your soul tribe without having to move around to all corners of the globe. In essence, instead of seeking out others of like mind, it is far more useful to attract those of like breath. When the inner harmony of one is breathed into awareness by the inner harmony of another, the gift of true intimacy is brought to life. It's quite natural to want others to confirm the gravity of your newfound freedom and expanded perspectives. And yet life surrounds you with people of varying levels of consciousness so you are able to cultivate compassion and mindfulness for everyone's relative standpoint, instead of being steeped in a community of similar thinking that tends to create the density of righteous belief.

Life is already an intentional community filled with infinite uniqueness honoring our one eternal truth masquerading in form. Some will see your light. Others will overlook it to the equal degree they see past the divinity within themselves. You don't need others to think like you in order to breathe into tangible form the most miraculous qualities, talents, and achievements only you were created to convey.

GOLDEN RULE #6

THE UNIVERSE *ALWAYS* HAS A PLAN

When I was in kindergarten, we were asked to draw a picture of what we wanted to be when we grew up. I hadn't given it much thought, and I just drew the first thing that came to mind. Apparently, it was so distressing to my teacher that my parents were called in for a meeting.

When they arrived, my teacher showed my parents the pictures the kids drew—a fireman, an astronaut, even the president. Then she pointed to my picture and asked: "What do you make of this?"

My mom responded, "Knowing my son, there is probably a very good reason why he drew this picture."

So I was called in from recess, and standing before my teacher and parents, I said, "When I grow up, I want to be the garbage man."

"Why the garbage man?" they asked.

Without even missing a beat, I just looked at them and said, "Because they only work on Fridays."

My teacher and parents were doing their best to hold back their endearing laughter as my mom informed me, "No, Matthew. They only work on Fridays on our street." To which I responded, "Forget it then," running off, hoping to capture as much recess time that remained. Apparently, even in kindergarten, I was trying to figure out how to work the least number of hours! And yet the Universe had a plan for me. One that didn't fit into the conventional workforce options children often imagine. More of this plan became evident in sixth grade, when a classmate asked me what I wanted to be when I grew up. I remember hearing it rained a lot in Seattle, and I'd always had a fantasy about living somewhere it rains on a regular basis. I had also loved creative writing, so I said, "I will live in Seattle, writing my best-selling books." I remember the kid looking at me, in awe of my confidence, unsure if it was prophetic or delusional. If we fast-forward my life 28 years, I am an author of two best-selling books that were both written in Seattle, where I've lived for the past 13 years.

This was a plan the Universe always had for me. Although I didn't know I'd be writing spiritual books, that such a career as a healer even existed, all of that would be revealed in time. While I had glimpses throughout my life of where I was headed, I was always being guided by an intuitive force of inner-knowing: an unexplainable will of clarity that knew exactly what needed to be known. Looking back, I always knew there was a plan for me, just as the Universe always has a plan for you.

This is why the sixth Golden Rule reminds you: *"The Universe* always *has a plan."* It is a plan you are always fulfilling—no matter the choices made along the way.

THE PURPOSE OF TIME

All too often, what gets in the way of you knowing the Universe has a plan is also one of the ego's mortal enemies. To make things even more difficult for ego, its mortal enemy is one of the soul's greatest allies. It is the dimension of *time*. When lost in time, you often have the dilemma of everything you want seeming so far away, while you're unable to get away from the things you don't want to experience.

The ego often wonders, "Why do I get more time with the things I don't want and so little time with the things I do want?" It is through the gift of time that you are able to measure how much or how little ego remains by how often disharmony arises in your experience.

You may ask yourself: How easily can I be frustrated? How impatient can I be? Such questions help you determine the type of relationship you have with time. Once your relationship with time is centered in true abiding harmony, then you are given access to understanding reality as a co-creative process. While there is a law of attraction, it is essential to understand it from a heart-centered perspective. In the old paradigm, the antiquated way of teaching the law of attraction certainly felt exciting, but it didn't quite amount to bringing you the things you were eager to manifest. This is because in the old way, you're often trying to manifest a different reality by being in *opposition* with time. You're trying to create something that isn't here right now. From the soul's perspective, the law of attraction is a chance to say, "I accept that my desire confirms that what I want is somewhere up ahead waiting for me. I acknowledge my desire as a sneak preview that I'm being prepared to receive. Perhaps the reason I don't have what I want right now is because I'm developing the worthiness to handle having it. Thank you, Universe, for this time to prepare as I open up to being a more worthy receiver. Thank you for the gift of time."

Your desire for what you want is remembering what's already been created. Throughout the dimension of time, you are preparing to receive at a higher level by cultivating the maturity and worthiness to *actually have* what you want, without slowing or stalling the trajectory of your ever-growing expansion. If you got what you wanted at the wrong time, it would stunt your growth by distracting you with shiny new objects. The Universe has to give you what you want, but in a way that complements and continues your rate of expansion. This is why everything happens over a period of time. If you could snap your fingers and heal right now, it would indicate that there was never a greater purpose for having something to heal.

Like the law of attraction, true healing isn't always a matter of getting what you want, but *receiving* all that you need to help you transform at your most optimal capacity. There's a certain amount of time you are meant to spend under specific personal conditions and various states of consciousness. By being at certain levels of consciousness for specific periods of time, you build up the necessary pressure to inspire the growth, and expansion, needed to guide you along to your next highest level of consciousness. This is why everything is the way it is.

Here's another way of looking at it: you aren't sad because you are an unhappy person. You are *experiencing sadness* as part of your healing journey, to create space for more light to be embodied. You will receive everything you desire at exactly the moment in time it is meant to arrive. Until that moment comes, any degree of sadness is a sacred stage of healing that is essentially making more space for happiness to dwell within you. The more space you create for more happiness to be, the greater happiness you are able to feel. Once happy, you are able to allow external creations to come as they will without defining new people, places, and things as a promise of greater happiness. Sadness is a catalyst of healing that makes space for true happiness to emerge.

The law of attraction means the law. The law means a truth that is never false. The law of attraction is you are always attracting *exactly* what you need to become who you were born to be. Whether you have manifested everything you've wanted, or are still waiting for the payout, here is an amazing discovery to uncover. Try repeating these words out loud:

If at this moment
I had everything I ever wanted,
I'd feel exactly the same as I do right now.

From this space, you are no longer under the impression that new people, places, or things are going to change how you feel. In the new spiritual paradigm, your feelings change as healing occurs, which unfolds with flawless precision when you allow yourself to heal openly and authentically. As you allow the Universe to hold the vision of life's greatest plan, you are strengthening the attribute of faith.

Faith is a willingness to let go by *making peace with time*. It is relaxing, unpacking your bags, and turning wherever you are into a home. Even if displaced miles away from your desired destination, faith says, "Everything's okay." The ego contends with the wisdom of faith by asking, "How can it be okay if it's not what I want?" The soul already knows everything is okay, whether you have what you want or not. Wanting is a sneak preview of what's coming your way. It's not a reward or a punishment; it's the Universe preparing you to handle the gravity of having your deepest desires fulfilled. While it is common for the ego to believe it cannot feel better until external circumstances become better, through the eyes of the Universe, it is healthy to desire as a way of getting excited for what's on the distant or not-too-distant horizon of your experience.

When grounded in the wisdom of the soul, you can embrace your desires as a part of the plan the Universe has for you without holding out for such creations as the only way to get excited about life. While the ego maintains this type of standoff with the Universe, it is all a part of the ego's letting go process, which cannot be rushed or forced, but welcomed through the cultivation of faith. In faith, we realize the ego mainly wants what it doesn't have—simply because it doesn't have it. Once it gets what it previously didn't have, the ego shifts its focus to *something else* it doesn't have and continues its never-ending standoff with the Universe. While this is all happening, the Universe holds loving space for the ego to let go, knowing getting what you want never changes how you feel. It is just a subtle way of fighting with time. In order to make peace with time, it is important to use your time wisely through the cultivation of faith. In doing so, you activate the true law of attraction from a more heart-centered space.

As auspicious as it sounds, in order to activate the true law of attraction, you must venture *beyond* your understanding of it.

BEYOND THE LAW OF ATTRACTION

What if the plan the Universe has for you is so extraordinary, so miraculous, so unthinkably precise, that it is *beyond* your ability to visualize it in any way, shape, or form? What if the reason why you can't envision what you want, or why you don't know what you desire, is because everything that's already coming your way is *beyond* your wildest imagination?

In the art of letting go, it is far more helpful to go there, instead of holding out hope for one finite outcome or static conclusion. This is what it means to go *beyond* the law of attraction. In order to venture beyond it, you must explore the highest way of understanding the co-creative process. Co-creation is the marriage between destiny and free will. Destiny knows everything is meant to be, while free will understands the unique journey you are exploring, in order to fulfill your destiny, is based on the freedom of options available to you. It's not one way or another, but a marriage of both—intertwined as one.

To really understand the law of attraction from the soul's perspective, let me share an experience I had. I remember driving to the grocery store one afternoon, and saying to myself, "I will have a parking spot waiting for me in the front of the store!" As

I pulled into the parking lot, I immediately noticed a car pulling out right up front. I thought, *I did it. Thank you, parking angels!* As I pulled into the front spot, my guides offered me a vision. I was shown the exact same scenario from a parallel dimension. In this dimension, I didn't declare any intention for the front spot, and yet I still got the same parking spot—just seeing it as a moment of surprising fortune. In both examples I wound up getting the same parking space, but in the dimension I was inhabiting, there was still a belief that I had to will the spot to me.

I then realized that my declaration was only a reminder of the parking space that was waiting for me. It wasn't as if the parking space didn't exist before I declared it. It was already meant to be. There are many of us who have made bold declarations to manifest specific outcomes into reality. Often times, we declare life will be a specific way. And when it doesn't unfold as planned, we either think the law of attraction is phony or we use it to get down on ourselves for not being able to attract our desires on command. As I've stated earlier, every desire is a sneak preview of a reality awaiting your arrival. Each outcome coming your way is cross-referenced by the emotion you imagine feeling, once the thing you are hoping to attract arrives. Let's say you envision a different romantic partner. From the perspective of your vision, you are picturing the qualities and attributes of who you'd like to call into your reality. As you envision this new romance, a feeling of fulfillment *engulfs* your senses. As this occurs, the Universe takes a snapshot of your vision and searches through the infinite potential of parallel dimensions to deliver you into a reality that allows you to feel as fulfilled as you envisioned feeling. It may include a new partner, or an entirely different scenario, where you are able to feel as fulfilled as you envisioned feeling, but throughout a set of circumstances more aligned with your soul's path.

The ego hears this and gets intimidated by the notion of being able to feel as you desire without it requiring life to give you the circumstances you crave. Again, from the perspective of ego, it can only envision feeling different within the construct of a different reality. One of the ego's core beliefs is: "I can't be happy here." This is because the ego is not equipped to exist in the present moment, which is the only place happiness exists. If the ego stopped for more than a few minutes to observe the present moment, it would begin unraveling and integrate into the light. Inevitably, the ego does let go into the light, but it requires your physical relaxation and heart-centeredness to help it feel safe enough to be set free.

From the soul's perspective, whether the pictures held in mind match the outcomes you are attracting or not, it rejoices in the grace of Universal magic that will always help you feel the exact emotions you desire. Even if the very things you want don't seem to show up, the soul thanks the Universe for helping to loosen the grip of personal attachment. You may not immediately get what you want, but you will always get exactly what you need, whether to help you see through one of the ego's core limiting beliefs or to inspire a series of emotional reactions that would have otherwise stayed dormant and unhealed.

When you are aligned with your soul, you create a harmonious relationship with time. This type of harmony is called "being in the flow." Whether your ego tends to crave the outcomes that are always far off in the distance, or your soul inspires you to only want the things that are unfolding before you, you are always on a trajectory to feeling the way you desire throughout the Universe's plan. It may not be the news your ego wants to hear, but it could only be the exact wisdom you need.

EXERCISE: Letting Go of Attachment

Write down all the things you want to attract. As you do this, pinpoint the *exact* emotions you would feel when those realities take shape in your life. Acknowledge that no matter what is meant to be, you are always destined to feel as you desire, since well-being is an attribute of your awakening soul.

Now, take the next step into alignment with the Universe by asking: "If these things don't immediately manifest, what are the gifts of *not* getting what I want?" Imagine the possibilities that might exist for you.

For example, if you envision a newer reality that makes you feel fulfilled, then not getting what you want is a perfect way to face and heal the opposite vibration of discontent. As layers of discontent are healed, greater space for fulfillment arises, whether bringing you everything you've envisioned or under more surprising circumstances. Such an experience not only escorts you beyond the law of attraction, but also beyond the limiting viewpoint of your ego.

YOUR MANTRA FOR RULE #6

To embody the wisdom of Golden Rule #6, please read or recite out loud the following words:

The Universe always has a plan—no matter how anything seems to be.

As you will continue to see, life has a plan for you and has since the beginning of time. When you're in ego, there are two plans: what you want, and what life has in store for you. Once aligned with the soul, there's only one plan. Even when unexpected things happen—*you always get your way.*

SPIRITUAL MYTH-BUSTING: "If it is to be, it's always up to me."

The ego thinks in extremes: if it's all predestined, the ego is likely to sit back and wait for life to change, only to grow more frustrated when new things don't unfold. If it's all a matter of free will, the ego adopts a belief suggesting, "It cannot be unless it's up to me."

As always, the truth exists somewhere in the middle. Yes, destiny shall always unfold, but your choices are determining how direct or circuitous of a path it takes to get from point A to B. While your participation is necessary, it doesn't require exhaustive effort, or pushing against anything, in order to play your part.

If the way in which you participate in the unfolding of your destiny seems exhausting or overwhelming, try making choices from a space of renewed faith and boundless courage, *without* attachments to the outcome. When you are able to work in collaboration with the hands of fate without a constant fixation on the circumstances you desire, you are able to be transformed over a period of time to fulfill the will of the Universe—countless lifetimes in the making. There is a destiny. It is guaranteed, and it also requires your participation. It may include outcomes the ego may desire, but it can only be fulfilled by the light of your soul.

From this depth of understanding, you develop great respect for the role of the ego that must let go in order for your highest potential to be. You are able to thank the ego for the gift of letting go, as you discover all the ways you can participate in the evolution of your journey, but from a space that is always aligned with the truth of heart-centered consciousness. This is the heart of inspired action.

GOLDEN RULE #7

EVERYTHING CHANGES, BUT IT CAN ONLY CHANGE YOU FOR THE BETTER

Since I was about 12 years old, I have been searching for my wife. While navigating the terrain of hormones and fumbling my way through social interactions, I regularly fantasized about the woman I would someday marry. The one with whom I would have the honor of being called her adoring husband. About 27 years later, I would have the privilege of meeting the most incredible woman. Her beauty captivated my senses, her grace engulfed my spirit, and her charm delighted every cell of my body. I told myself the moment we met, "I will do anything to be with her." And so our courtship began. From long-distance dating to moving in together and then a marriage. It was every bit as magical as I had imagined it would be from a very early age.

Often in marriages, patterns and routines develop. As much as both of us tried not to play these roles, it was impossible to avoid. There was never a single argument or moment of discord—just two different energy fields attempting to harmonize in rhythm, only to bump and collide more often than align. We both loved each other so deeply, and yet the romance would come and go like a fleeting seasonal harvest. Our relationship ended, then we came back together, hoping we had healed whatever was causing our romance to erode and dissolve. After coming back together three times, the mystery of our dance was solved. We stayed the course, remained true to the process, and out of this journey birthed a soulful friendship that no desire for romance could deny. I thought it was the love I had been waiting for, and it turned out to be an even better dose of healing I didn't know I needed.

Of course, there were incredible levels of pain, loss, and grief. These came and went like waves of helplessness that would horrifically crash upon my heart, breaking me open wider each and every time. It felt like the cells of my body were on fire. I felt lost and bewildered, having lost a part of my identity that I had waited a lifetime for.

There were stages of disbelief ("What did I do to upset the Universe in order to be punished like this?"), then bargaining ("What must I quickly learn in order to not attract this again?"), all leading up to full-blown implosion.

When transformation goes this deep, it's not a moment where you casually acknowledge the importance of surrender. You're being pulled into the deepest surrender that cannot be resisted, avoided, or outrun.

The end of my marriage was devastating and humbling. Ultimately, it was liberating. My heart has never felt so pure with the utmost pride and respect for the man I am now.

Our journey of emotional freedom brings us to the seventh Golden Rule: *"Everything changes, but it can only change you for the better."*

Why does true, abiding happiness come from within? Because everything changes. If your happiness is defined by outside things, then your happiness is like an emotional stock portfolio governed by the movement of your personal markets. Self-worth goes up, and it crashes and plummets, based on the circumstantial movement of your personal reality.

While life conspires to always change from one form to another, the law of reality is that anything and everything can only change you for the better. It may not change your circumstances into better circumstances, but it's always guaranteed to change *you* into a better version of yourself. This is evolution's timeless guarantee. While circumstances don't always immediately improve, *you* always get better.

When you really internalize this rule, you become a conscious participant in life. That's when you start to really accept the deeper invitations into the heart of surrender. Surrender is not sitting on the couch waiting for life to do it for you. Surrender is facing what you encounter, opening up, receiving what is given, and knowing it will only make you better because that is life's only option. You can't go backward. You can only stay exactly where you're at until you are ready to step forward into the destiny of your true glory and greatness. Best of all, you don't have to wonder what series of events you might need in order to become this highest you. All you need is to be willing to stay the course by letting go and loving yourself throughout each twist and turn.

In order to become a willing participant, you have to know what it means to be an *unwilling* participant.

An unwilling participant is one who is attempting to avoid the gravity of surrender, who is negotiating with life instead of opening to it. In the old spiritual paradigm, it would be seen as a form of contemplation. But in order for true insight to dawn, we must ask how our lives are only changing us for the better with no further negotiations in mind. Within this Golden Rule is the opportunity to discover meditation from a different perspective. Oftentimes, when we try to meditate, we likely find a quiet space, close our eyes, and begin negotiating for more preferable circumstances. Meditation is *not* negotiation. Meditation is what happens when negotiation dissolves. Negotiating with life is to assume that what's happening is a mistake. Remember Golden Rule #6, "the Universe always has a plan." If the Universe always has a plan, then any form of negotiating could only veer you off your highest path.

When you are embodying this Golden Rule, you are cultivating the soul's attribute of stillness. The ego lives to negotiate, but the ego isn't capable of being still. This is why if your ego is attempting to meditate, it's likely an internal negotiation with the beauty of empty space.

EXERCISE: Being Meditated

In order to cultivate the quality of stillness, I want to give you the experience of being meditated instead of someone trying to achieve a state of meditation.

As stillness is cultivated, you want to allow the meditation to be done *to* you. All you need to do is sit and simply listen. You may hear sounds to confirm that you're listening. Even if you don't hear anything, the fact that you hear nothing means listening remains active. Whether you hear something or nothing, listening is always an uninterrupted state of being known as *stillness*.

To deepen your awareness of stillness, please repeat these words out loud:

I am stillness itself,
not the one trying to be still.
And anything that seems to disrupt stillness
is simply the experience
stillness is noticing.
Just like
no noise interrupts listening,
noise is simply what listening listens to.
And even when there's nothing to hear
it's only noticeable
'cause listening continues.
Only stillness is the listener.
And because I am the one listening,
stillness could only be

WHAT I AM.

YOUR MANTRA FOR RULE #7

I can see how everything changes me for the better whenever I am still.

ADVERSITY AND INCONVENIENCE

When adversity enters your life, what is really happening? Adversity is often how you interpret change or loss. When the perception of adversity strikes, it means your current rhythm has been disrupted to let you know it's time to grow and expand to the next level. When this happens, that jarring rhythmic disruption simultaneously expands the light of your soul, while also triggering your ego. As you become more emotionally free, you are more aware of how often the soul expands, instead of feeling overwhelmed by the reactive nature of your ego.

I remember many years ago, I was in the airport waiting for a flight. The person in front of me was talking to the ticket agent. To his horror, he arrived a few minutes too late and wasn't allowed to board the plane.

"I'm supposed to be on that plane," he said.

The ticket agent said, "The door is closed—you're gonna have to be on the next flight."

To which he replied, "But that's gonna make me late to where I need to go."

This is an example of a jarring rhythmic disruption we commonly perceive as adversity. Sure, the change of plans will guide him along a path of greater expansion, but before he arrives, he is facing the part of his ego being triggered by the process. If this happens to you, yes, your entire day is now different. The way it was supposed to be has now been categorically altered. What does that amount to? A series of inconveniences. At the end of the day, your biggest problem with inconvenience is you are being forced to spend more time where you did not plan to be. Still, you have the ability to go where you need to go, just not in the way that you had planned or imagined. Your way became *life's* way, and life had far different plans than you had. It happens to the best of us.

As a result of being in a position of spending more time where you didn't plan to be, believe it or not, you've received a gift. You're going to be where you didn't plan to be, around people you didn't plan to be around, and you'll have the opportunity to become better as a result. The question is—are you willing to fully participate in life's plan for you? When you are living from the light of your soul, inconvenience can be unexpected, but it's more hilarious than it is harmful. I'll give you another example.

A year or so ago, I began watching the NBC show *This Is Us*. I was hooked. Every week, I couldn't wait for the episode to come on. I'd even have a three-day countdown. Check the calendar. What day is it? Oh my God, one day until *This Is Us* is on. At that time, it was building up to a season finale. Finally, I arrived at two minutes before the show. The show was getting ready to come on and my cable went out. It was as if my cable box decided it was done serving me. Here I was, looking forward to this show for *days*.

I took a deep breath. Then, I laughed. I thought to myself, *Well, there's that. Apparently, I'll watch it some other time*. I decided to take a walk instead.

When you are emotionally free, when you are the light of your soul, you can look forward to something for days, even *years*, but it is all grounded in the maturity of surrender. As this depth of maturity awakens in you, your relationship with inconvenience is more of an ally than an enemy. I wasn't glad that it happened, but no harm was done to me. I had thought that from 8:00 to 9:00 p.m. on that night I'd be watching my favorite show, and life had a different plan. It didn't even strike me as inconvenient. It struck me as unexpected. That's all it was—unexpected change. Wow, I get to spend time doing what I didn't plan to do. No negotiation necessary.

You know what I didn't do when my cable went out? I didn't blame myself. In Golden Rule #2, we learned that anyone who blames you isn't happy. So now we deepen that insight by not blaming ourselves for the way things unfold. Sometimes, when we rationalize things, we blame ourselves. "Oh, I know why this happened. I should have gotten the other cable plan." It's usually something you think you did wrong. This is why Golden Rule #1 is "You've done nothing wrong."

What is it like in this moment to not blame yourself for *anything*? What if you no longer use the soul's journey to find spiritual ways to blame at all? Oh my God, my cable went out. What happened to my vibration? Did I not have tonight's episode on my vision board? Did my cable go out from empathing the people who don't have cable?

What is it like to not blame the ego for anything? What is it like to not blame your shadow for anything? What is it like to not blame the collective unconsciousness for anything? What is it like to blame *nothing or anyone at all*?

If there's any tendency to blame, you're already in a state of negotiation, because negotiation begins with the assignment of blame. You're only negotiating out of something that you feel you're being punished by, and in that, you're unaware that everything is here to help you. More than likely, you're trying to negotiate out of an opportunity to be more still in an environment where you get to spend more time being where you didn't plan to be. The only example where this doesn't directly apply is in toxic environments or abusive relationships. If your innocence is being disrespected, suppressed, dominated, or overpowered, any form of inner or outer negotiation just makes you an accomplice to the crimes committed against you. Yes, you will heal and be an even better version of yourself than you could possibly imagine. But in order to facilitate this growth, you must say no to abusive environments and toxic relationships so you can find the inner resolve and outer safety where true stillness can blossom.

When we meditate, typically we're meditating under the most ideal conditions. You've blocked out some time in your day from work or family commitments. You're in the comfort of your home or at a yoga studio, filled with incense and soothing music. You're in a comfortable posture, feeling relaxed. But how does that prepare you to be in harmony when life becomes less than ideal? It's one thing to be at peace and totally still when you've prepared to stop. But the *real* measurement is how peaceful you are when you are stopped abruptly while in motion. During any state of disruption, your nervous system has to go from movement to stillness, and that change will show how much ego remains to be integrated.

As you cultivate stillness, you are able to freely go from being in motion to unexpected stillness, from chaotic, external situations to inner peace. You're able to weather the storm, to accept when there are unexpected changes between your personal plan and the unique journey life has in store for you.

CLOSED-EYE VS. OPEN-EYE MEDITATION

Meditation can't just be a practice employed under the most perfect set of circumstances. It must possess the ability to be applied throughout your life, at a moment's notice. Closed-eye meditation is what we commonly think of when we imagine meditation. It's wonderful. I've meditated with my eyes closed for most of my life, but in recent years, I've begun doing open-eye meditation.

Closed-eye meditation helps you strengthen harmony with closed-eye experiences. But wouldn't you agree that most of the experiences in your life that disrupt you occur when your eyes are *open*? If most of your moments of being triggered occur when your eyes are *open*, then your most functional approach to meditation has to be done as an open-eye experience. Through an open-eye meditation practice, you will find that when your eyes are open in everyday life, you will be triggered less and less by any form of inconvenience.

If you can't sleep at night, then closed-eye meditation would be perfect. But, if like most people, your disharmony is during open-eye experiences, then try meditating with eyes open and see how quickly relief may come. Simply sit, be still, face forward, and listen. From this space, being stuck in traffic, missing a flight, or waiting in line won't throw you off—it will just be a different meditation to embrace.

SPIRITUAL MYTH-BUSTING: "Unexpected outcomes are how the Universe punishes you for past mistakes."

No matter how much we think we know better, it only takes a series of surprising occurrences or a consecutive number of setbacks to make you question what you've done wrong to earn this imagined form of karmic punishment. Because we live in an all-knowing and all-loving Universe, nothing occurs to punish us for the very experiences we incarnated to act out and learn from. We may believe we are being punished. While the ego believes pleasure can exist only beyond the threshold of pain, the soul knows degrees of pain and pleasure often exist in the same exact space.

What we often experience as pain is mainly how our nervous systems interpret rhythmic disruptions. This is where we go from the momentum of doing to the stillness of being so suddenly that it jars our innocence. As our nervous systems relax through the path of emotional freedom, sudden loss or unexpected change doesn't have to feel so damaging. When not so assaulting on your senses, it's easier to see the gift each experience provides, instead of seeing it as any form of punishment. While sudden loss, unexpected change, or even a surprising turn of events doesn't have to be seen as *joyful*, you will be able to see how true, long-lasting happiness doesn't have to be disrupted when unexpected changes occur. It's simply a mirror of your own depth of adaptability. The more able you are to adapt to change and flow in the direction life is guiding you, the more rewarding your evolution becomes with less time spent perceiving life as any form of punishment. Why would you be punished for playing the exact role that gives you the amount of experiences you need in order to evolve from great to greater and beyond? Why is the Universe only supporting you when life goes your way? Where is the unwavering trust in a higher knowing beyond the ups and downs of gain or loss?

From the soul's perspective, we accept that life could only change in whatever way helps us sharpen our ethics and cultivate deeper values. It doesn't have to be a popular experience to be the everything you need to shine brighter than you could possibly imagine. From this perspective, you cultivate an inner radiance to serve those still finding their way out of the despair of blame, scarcity, and victimhood.

You are never being punished by life, and your manifestation skills aren't broken. You are simply seeing each moment through, from start to finish, while becoming the embodied essence that attracted you to the beauty of this exact incarnation.

GOLDEN RULE #8

IN ORDER TO BE EMOTIONALLY FREE, IT'S OKAY TO DISLIKE

The modern-day spiritual journey is made up of equal parts insight and authenticity. This means you can't be so insightful that you forget to hold your ground for what is most meaningful to your heart, just as you cannot project your truths onto others—no matter how clear you think you're being. A soul cannot evolve without the human vessel to grow within, and the human vessel cannot function without the fuel of your soul's essence. It is a marriage of two seemingly opposite aspects merging together as One, the more often you show both sides equal respect and importance.

While my spiritual growth has been birthed out of the difficulties I've been so blessed to face, it doesn't take away from the *equally* valid human experience woven throughout every trial, tribulation, breakdown, breakthrough, failure, and success. My co-dependent childhood may have been a training ground for my expansion, and for all the lives I've helped to heal, but it doesn't discount the heartache, betrayal, and bewilderment I endured. I may have used my experiences of being bullied as a launching pad into greater levels of mindfulness, but that doesn't take away the nights I cried myself to sleep. I may have an innate spiritual gift of knowing the life that exists beyond the doorway of death, but it didn't make it any less intense when I was helping my relatives cross over while surrounded by loved ones who were nearing their personal breaking point.

I may have glimpsed greater spiritual truths by questioning the narratives at Sunday school, but it didn't change how resentful I felt for being forced to study something that wasn't in my heart. I may have had visions of my future and somehow followed each breadcrumb to live a life of everlasting fulfillment, but it doesn't change how *uncertain* I felt in getting there, or how afraid I was of failing.

I may have experienced the deepest transformation of a lifetime as a result of my marriage, but it doesn't change how earth-shatteringly painful it was navigating the terrain of a heart broken wide open.

Perhaps I am able to see the wisdom in such difficult experiences and view from an expanded spiritual perspective, simply because my human experience has never been diminished or discounted by the clarity in view. The essence of being spiritual is learning how to be consciously human. Meanwhile your human reality transforms into a vivid spiritual adventure as you embrace the wisdom of an ever-loving Universe. This is what it means to be embodied, integrated, and emotionally free. These are the gifts received when learning to let go.

To take the next step, we come upon the eighth Golden Rule: *"In order to be emotionally free, it's okay to dislike."*

In the previous rules, you've learned how the Universe always has a plan, how everything changes, but it can only change you for the better. Now let's add on to that an insightful reminder: you don't have to like it. It's okay to dislike.

I think it's a very common misunderstanding that in order to embody love, you have to like everything and everyone. One of the most common misunderstandings is when the ego is trying to attain perfection on the spiritual journey, the conflict is that it's trying to like an experience that isn't trying to be liked in your reality. When adversity arises in your experience, it has a job to do. Its mission is to evolve you to the next highest level of consciousness. It is designed to help you grow. It's not asking to be liked. All too often, the ego believes, "If I can learn to like my experiences, I'll probably be in less pain."

It's a well-intended aspiration, but instead of trying to blindly embrace your experiences, it's far more useful to move with the current of reality fueled by the grace of personal integrity. In the new spiritual paradigm, you learn to be in harmony with life simply by not obligating yourself to like what's happening.

Dislike is the recognition that you are acknowledging something that seems foreign to your core values. To dislike someone's behavior is because they may be acting in a way that is not an expression of the ideals and ethics you hold to be true. If your deepest core value is unconditional love and someone is not treating you in an unconditionally loving way, your dislike is recognizing that they're acting from a vibration that you do not resonate with. That's called discernment. It's not actually a judgment. Judgment is when you criticize, condemn, and define someone permanently as a result of differences in behavior or perception.

Dislike is just a momentary way of becoming aware of the authenticity of your experience. I'm here to remind you, in order to be emotionally free, it's okay to dislike. If you try to tell yourself that you cannot dislike because that's not what it means to be a *perfectly* evolved spiritual being, you're holding yourself accountable to an impossible criteria of expectations and standards.

You are not here to be perfect. You're here to embrace how perfect you already are. The most direct way to understand how perfect you already are is to embrace the *authenticity* of your subjective experience. Don't try to like what you already dislike. Give yourself the right to dislike whatever bothers you, what captures your attention that does not match the deepest values you hold to be true.

If you see a political figure abusing power, allow yourself to feel what it instigates on an emotional level. If movies like *Schindler's List* devastate you to your core, allow that devastation to be felt. There are countless souls who selflessly incarnated to perish tragically, just to be a part of a bigger wake-up call that activates the consciousness of a spiritually evolving species. No matter what depth of unimaginable cruelty drops you to your knees and twists your stomach into knots, allow each sensation to be a catalyst of our own transformation, instead of reflecting back the same unconsciousness by judging the actions of others. The first step is to feel as deeply and openly as possible. In order to do so, it's okay to dislike.

EXERCISE: Permission to Dislike

Can you take one moment and give yourself the right to dislike something? Notice what happens. Maybe you start smiling. If so, it's because when I gave you permission to dislike, you instantly shifted into a state of harmony. Do you know what the harmony you felt in your body was? A state of *true acceptance*. To actually be yourself, by reserving the right to just be honest. It's such a clarifying moment of relief when shifting into the authenticity of the soul where it's okay to dislike.

Dislike doesn't have to lead to violence, judgment, condemnation, ridicule, resentment, or cruelty. It can actually inspire a greater response of noble behavior if you give yourself the right to just *feel how you feel*.

ACCEPTANCE AND DISCERNMENT

True acceptance doesn't require effort; it's just confessing the gravity of your most honest experience.

I remember my parents used to take me to the ice-cream store as a reward for a job well done, after a baseball game or a good score on a test. As a kid, what's more fun than sampling all the flavors? I would sample each and every one until I found the taste combination I enjoyed the most. In order for me to decide which one I enjoyed the most, there had to have been flavors that *weren't* the ones I totally loved. Now as a kid, I was a fan of anything that had chocolate with peanut butter, cake pieces, and even pretzels. Basically, the ice cream flavor that had the most stuff in it. The one that barely even looked like ice cream because there were so many ingredients. That's what I wanted! The ones I liked the least were the fruit-flavored ones that to my young palate tasted boring: lemon, orange, raspberry, especially sherbet. I mean, what is that?

The one thing I never did when I was at the ice-cream store is feel bad about the flavors I liked the least. I never thought I was hurting their feelings. I only appreciated that I got to try all the flavors so I could figure out what I enjoyed the most.

Let's apply this to your spiritual journey: you have the permission to sample *all of the experiences*, all the vibrations, all the various combinations of experience. In order for you to actually find the things you want to embrace and resonate with, you have to also encounter things that you don't respond well to. This helps you develop the skill of *discernment*.

Somewhere along the spiritual journey, there was a secret memo that went out that said, "If you're a spiritual being, you're not allowed to have an opinion. Since we're all one, no one gets to be an individual." Let's unravel this misconception, because a true heart-centered spiritual journey is about being an individuated expression of your divine consciousness. It is where you are one with all that is, while also standing for everything that you hold near and dear to your heart. Just because you like something and dislike something else doesn't mean that anything is being judged as less than; it's just you appreciating the fact that life is giving you a chance to figure out what you uniquely resonate with. This won't turn you into a negative person. Quite the opposite; the more you dislike, the more it evaporates out of your field. If you have the right to dislike it, it will rarely show up. The gift of dislike is you are only disliking what is helping you draw your attention toward the things that are really resonant with you.

Once you are clear on what resonates, you become very decisive as a human being. Simply put, in order to receive your highest potential, you have to be discerning. Not everything will be a yes or meant to be chosen by you. How else can each yes become powerful and unwavering, if you're not able to stand in the truth of every no?

I'm not saying to lead with dislike, but to accept when it comes up for you.

In order to have a direct experience of this insight, try repeating these words out loud:

I allow the one
who is capable of dislike
to be accepted and loved as never before,
contrary to my past.
I do not
require this one within me
to always be on their best behavior,
trying to earn my loving attention.
When as a child,
that was the very game
I never seemed to have won.
And instead what's occurring
is that I am facing my own conditioned
nature.
It has the right to lash out,

based on the attention it never received.
It has the right to use thoughts
to dislike anything in existence.
And my job
is to meet that dislike
and any form of discord
as an opportunity
to love and accept myself as never before.
Simply because
dislike
is giving the part of me
that felt suppressed and silenced by my past
the right to speak
anything it wants on the inside
with no punishment coming its way
and only greater acceptance and love to be offered.
What dislike suggests
may not always be the clearest truth,
but the opportunity is always clear and available
to use any internal experience of dislike
as an opportunity
to love and accept the parts of myself
shut down by the judgment of others.

As it's been said over many, many lifetimes, with great power comes great responsibility. With that said, do you know that you already possess the responsibility to handle the power of dislike and to do great things with it? Maybe the greatest thing you can do with dislike is to not only be discerning and clear in what you resonate with, but to love, adore, and heal the most damaged, hurtful parts of yourself. The moment dislike happens, now you know where to send more kindness. Now you know where greater self-care needs to go. Now you know where greater acceptance is required. And you'll find that in dislike, you have an innocence that is trying to prove that it lives within a universe of unconditional love. It just wants the right to think and act differently just to see for itself that no punishment will be handed down.

This is why in Golden Rule #8, when I say in order to be emotionally free it's okay to dislike, you are cultivating the soul's attribute of acceptance. Accepting the deepest purpose of dislike is an opportunity to commune with your hurt, damaged aspects of self and to meet those parts who use dislike as an attention-seeking device, begging for the healing resolve of your most tender attention and affection. The first level of dislike is giving yourself the permission to be discerning in your choices. The deeper invitation is to recognize dislike as a chance to bring the gift of self-acceptance to your most insufferable rebellious parts. Beyond this inner emotional process, if a moment of dislike leads to creating solutions to remedy the plight of broken political and socioeconomic systems, it can only positively affect the sum of the whole. All of these benefits and opportunities could never be made possible if believing dislike is wrong to experience.

YOUR MANTRA FOR RULE #8

When it's okay to dislike, you are able to access the attribute of true self-acceptance. This leads you to the mantra of acceptance. It's two of the most powerful words your heart yearns to hear:

It's okay.

Simply repeat this mantra to your heart for 1 to 3 minutes at a time. How does it feel? How does it affect your nervous system? How much quieter is your mind? Can you sense less physical tension—no matter the circumstances in view?

SPIRITUAL MYTH-BUSTING: "Spiritual beings must like everything."

Just because divinity resides in every form, doesn't always mean it's trying to win a popularity contest. Yes, divinity is the light of all-knowing, all-loving truth, but only once it's fully realized. Much like children are more likely to act consistently mature once they reach adulthood, human beings become conscious vessels of Source energy as they evolve. Dislike doesn't mean you don't respect the divinity in another. Initially, it means you are not resonating with the very behavior that could only inspire greater expansion, once those hurtful parts in you are seen, acknowledged, and embraced.

Even when consistently treated poorly by someone, the gift of dislike ushers you toward the next milestone of courageous decision-making to move yourself out of any perceivable danger zone and into the safety of a more supportive environment. How could you have ever mustered the tenacity, drive, and determination to rescue yourself if you were not keenly aware of how much you disliked the abuse?

Attempting to like what triggers discord will only cultivate greater inner conflict.

If you tried to like the actions of a serial killer, you might be surprised to hear the Universe say, "That's not what we were trying to inspire in you right now." You might think, "But I honor the divine, no matter the form." And the Universe would say, "If you truly honored divinity, you'd respect the purpose of each form." You might imagine, "What would be the purpose of seeing the unthinkable actions of a serial killer?" To which the Universe would say, "To inspire the social justice and political reform that brings communities together in service for a greater good."

Sometimes you may try to like everything across the board because you don't like how it feels to dislike. And yet if you are outraged enough by the actions in view, you'll be inspired to do something that will bring greater resolve into the lives of others by serving the role the Universe has designed.

Spiritual beings can be thoughtful, inquisitive, and generous, but it tends to be a passive way of being. This doesn't mean to oscillate from passive to aggressive, but to *trust* in the clarity of dislike that might be setting the stage for you to inspire greater positive change in the world.

Spiritual evolution is not a "one size fits all" approach to life. If it were, you would be robbed of the beauty of thinking your way through situations and recognizing the heroic ways in which you can contribute to the evolution of every innocent heart.

Only an ego judging itself for the way it fails to behave believes it has to like everything across the board. In order to maintain respect for the divinity of all, while honoring the integrity any character is destined to play, simply bow to the dislike in view and say to it, "Thank you for calling me into greater service for all."

In the new spiritual paradigm, it can't be all divine and no human, just as there is no spiritual growth in an all human, no divine viewpoint. Instead, we respect the divinity in *ourselves* that came to this planet to choose boldly, equally honoring the divinity of those who inspire dislike, only to remind us of parts we have a chance to accept in ourselves.

While conflict doesn't ever lead to peace, in order to cultivate peace, you can't be afraid of conflict in any way. Equally so, in order to be the most loving, passion-driven person you were born to be, it's okay to dislike.

The nature of dislike doesn't take us out of spiritual alignment. It's often the most potent way to place you on your highest path that can heal your deepest wounds and positively affects others—when letting courage take the lead.

GOLDEN RULE #9

PROJECTING ANGER DRAINS YOU OF ENERGY

When my parents got angry, they typically suspended truth and reason until they blew off their steam. I quickly learned to maintain a certain amount of distance, since being in close range meant feeling like a sitting duck for whatever emotional destruction would occur whenever their anger surfaced. As I got older, I tried intervening. I even remember feeling so traumatized by hearing my parents scream at each other that I would interrupt their fight, often defending whichever one was being hurt. As I came to the rescue of one parent, the parent I was rescuing would then admonish me for talking back to an adult. The contradictions and unfairness infuriated me. I would have screaming matches with them, doing anything to show them the limitations of their patterning and behavior. In each and every instance, I would retreat to my room, sobbing in anger and misery, exhausted by the twelve-round emotional battle I was never equipped to win.

It took many years, but I gradually began to see how acting out any degree of anger was exhausting to my body and harmful to my heart. Once I was no longer hypnotized by the righteous viewpoint I needed someone else to see, I could finally see how my anger only hurt *me*. It also placed all my power in someone else's hands, requiring them to see my point of view so I could be released from the commitment to my anger. At a certain point, anger became optional and surfaced more infrequently the less and less I needed others to change to my liking in order to feel okay.

At this point it was okay to dislike, but it didn't have to instigate anger, since the change required was always within my will and not something I needed from someone else. If someone upset me, I could either say something or walk away. If it continued, I could question whether this person should be in such close proximity to my innocence. Maybe it's a sign that our journey is complete and it's time to go our separate ways. In any event, the more options

I had, the less angry I became as a result of dislike. This also allowed me to hold loving space for my parents and their journey of growth. I would be able to see how their perceived anger was their frustration with themselves, not knowing how to access the options and choices that were already living within their hearts.

My parents never gave themselves any other option but to explode their anger onto others around them. As a result, they navigated the last chapter of their lives in states of medical debilitation. They never saw how much energy their anger drained out of their bodies, and in the end, their declining health became a physical manifestation of their bodies' exhaustion. It also set the stage for a surrendering of control, as a sharp-witted mind unraveled within the confines of a dissolving physical body.

Watching my parents decline in health and hold space for their surrendering of control was like a telepathic form of forgiveness from both their hearts. No matter how unfairly they treated me, I knew the purpose of these patterns was for me to help their souls evolve by daring to be unlike them.

I didn't want to live a life of anger, righteousness, resentment, victimhood, or exhaustion. I also didn't want all the hurt I experienced with my parents to go in vain, so I knew I had to use it as inspiration to better myself. Once both of my parents crossed over into the afterlife, all the anger I had felt and carried just vanished. I didn't have to remember to not be angry. It just stopped happening.

In the last Golden Rule, we spoke of how dislike can help us be more discerning, revealing the parts of ourselves that beg for our acceptance and love, and perhaps even inspire heroic roles that bring greater resolve and consciousness to the planet. To further that, we go to the ninth Golden Rule, which acts as a counter-balance. It reminds you that *projecting anger drains you of energy.* It's okay to dislike, but when it becomes a projection of anger, it means you are allowing dislike to control you. If you project anger, no matter what the effect it has on others, it always drains you of energy.

As empaths or those who are sensitive to the energies and experiences of others, we tend to be exhausted, even when witnessing the anger of others. The reason why other people's anger can drain you of energy is because you're actually sensing how drained they are by *their* anger, even if and when they're not aware of it. Naturally, the next question is: How do you deal with the emotional density that manifests as anger in the most conscious way, so as not to be drained of energy or do harm unto others? The answer always comes in one of the soul's highest attributes and one of the most critical and undervalued tools on the spiritual journey: your *creativity*.

When spiritual aspirations are not balanced and grounded with constant creative expression, you become *imbalanced* in form. A soul needs to have the wisdom of spirituality and the expression of creativity in order to be whole, grounded, integrated, and complete. In every heart is an artist waiting to be born. Perhaps a spiritual journey is how the victim transforms into a hero, making sense of their own individual journey by giving rise to the expansion of their own inner artist.

The inner artist is the narrator of one's transition from victimhood to hero or from ego to soul. The inner artist says, "Here are the things I saw, felt, and survived, and here's how it made me better." Art is the inner narrator of your soul's evolution. The more aligned with creative expression you tend to be, the less angry you'll be or even drained by the anger of others. This is because the energy of anger is an eruption of unexpressed passion.

An artist is one who channels the light of their spirit into inspired creative form. In doing so, the passion of creative energy is always flowing. If someone's inner artist has yet to be discovered, there is no outlet for the energy of their emotional body to be channeled. This ferments inside someone's heart as repressed unexpressed passion. The more passion has been repressed, the angrier one is likely to be. When the arising of anger can be seen as an artistic crisis, you are likely to have more patience and empathy for those who feel it but have no creative place to channel it.

EXPRESSING YOUR INNER ARTIST

The question becomes—how do you use your creativity to deal with the anger inside of you that, as long as it festers, drains energy, and when projected, can do harm to others? Creativity, whether it's in a contemplation, a writing exercise, or another medium, can give you the freedom to express anger in a healthy, mindful way.

If you're angry with someone, you could try writing them a letter and not sending it. Hide your stamps. Put your phone on airplane mode. Write a letter that is so outrageous, it almost embarrasses you to put it on paper. When you have given yourself permission to just spare no expense in expressing your anger in the written word, whether on a computer or a piece of paper, get rid of it. This is how you release the energy.

If you're into ecstatic dance, you could dance out your anger. If you're an artist, you can paint out your anger. If you're a singer, you could sing out your anger. If there's anger within you, any form of creative expression will transfer it from your emotional body and return it back to Source.

Spiritual evolution is the act of bringing awareness to the energies and emotions within you, but it is *creativity* that teaches us how to express and release it.

By spending more time aligned with your inner artist, you are liberated from anger by letting creativity set you free—simply by giving a voice to the parts that have been silenced and disempowered some time before.

YOUR MANTRA FOR RULE #9

I am only as angry as I'm in need of creatively expressing myself.

EXERCISE: Breaking the Silence

What needs to be expressed by your inner artist? No matter how painful of a memory exists, is there something inside you that has to be heard?

> Instead of focusing on who did what, simply focus on how it made you feel. When you do so, you can actually unravel the repressed passion (called anger) to discover the deeper wounds that need the outlet of creative expression. Will you write out your feelings? Voice them through expressing primal sounds? Chant it out? Can it inspire a collage, a drawing, or even abstract finger painting? Do you need to write someone an uncensored letter that is only meant for your eyes to read? Is there a book waiting to be birthed within you where the arc of the main character's journey matches your history of pain?
>
> It doesn't actually matter the medium of your art. It just has to be a way for your inner artist to bridge the gap between victimhood and the redemptive hero you are becoming.

SETTING YOURSELF FREE

In the latter years of my mother's life, she said to me one day, in a rather debilitated state, "I'm sorry for anything I did that hurt you." I looked at my mother's face with profound empathy, seeing how she could barely face a percentage of some of the things she did. This is because I wasn't the only one manipulated by my mother's ego. My mother was too. I said to my mother, "Thank you for saying that, but I've already forgiven you, for everything you've done. Thank you for the journey you've put me on."

I stood so proudly in my mother's presence, using everything that was done to me that I never could understand, that caused me to question myself and feel so unworthy. For the first time in my life, I embodied my true power with no one to rescue or be rescued from. It was at this moment where my mother met her adult soon who was a helpless child no more. She said, "Sorry"; I said, "Thank you."

Even in her dying moments, it was my opportunity to take all the compassion, thoughtfulness, and patience that sometimes she didn't give to me, and make sure they were gifts I gave *her* as she transitioned. This is what I want for you. To no longer be drained of the repressed passion within you that just wants to birth an inner artist. An artist that wants the right to talk about, to write about, to express all of the pain it can no longer afford to carry. Whenever you employ the soul's attribute of creativity, you are dissolving cycles of abuse by no longer being silenced in the most conscious and heart-centered way.

SPIRITUAL MYTH-BUSTING:
"Other people always need to know my truth."

It is often a very knee-jerk and co-dependent impulse to assume the truths you uncover in yourself are applicable to others. Often times, we, as energetically sensitive beings, are so insecure, we need other people to agree with our viewpoints in order to know we are okay to think and feel the way we do. While you may have a truth to be shared, perhaps the one in need of sharing it is the most important person needing to hear it. Other people may have triggered such feelings, but ultimately, the question of personal empowerment asks you: "Now that you feel this way, how will you allow it to make you better?"

When a personal truth needs to be accepted by others, you are likely to act in a way that is no better than the actions triggering you. Even though the ego firmly believes the other person will change to your liking if they can just see your point of view, the true healing that comes from any personal sharing has to do with the fact that *you* expressed your truth, whether or not the one listening agreed or even heard you. Knowing that you are the one who must express your truths, no matter how it's perceived or received, you are able to convey such truths through a wide range of artistic mediums that require you to express what no one else may need to hear.

While there are moments of cathartic relief where you just need to get something off your chest and give feelings a voice, others can be invited to hold space for your process without having to be a focal point. As you learn to share your feelings without blaming others, while reserving the right to dislike without draining yourself of energy through the withholding of unexpressed passion, you allow your inner artist out to play in celebration of your soul's expansion. If you are so desperately in need of speaking your truth, then you are equally the most important person who needs to hear it.

GOLDEN RULE #10

LOVE IS YOUR LIBERATOR

Throughout the unfolding of my path, it became more and more obvious that love was the only option left. This occurred as disappointment continually showed me how no one else but me could ever meet me where I need to be met.

Once my needs became my hole to fill, I was freed from believing others were acting from any other motivation than the nature of *their* journey. This produced an inherent level of respect for each and every being, no matter how differently their actions were from mine. The love I required was no longer anyone else's problem to resolve; as a result, the notion of problem began dissolving from view. I was no longer seeing burden, conflict, pressure, or stress, but a world of innocent hearts hiding from their own love by trying to get it from another. This began my more intimate journey of freedom that took me deeper than any insight I had ever learned. I had been liberated by love, and through the wisdom of our final golden rule, so shall you be.

This Golden Rule is just as important as the first one. It's the cornerstone of the modern-day spiritual journey. The very awakener of heart-centered consciousness. The tenth Golden Rule says, *"Love is your liberator."*

Notice how it says *love* is your liberator and not *other people* are your liberators. When love is your liberator, it is only the love that you cultivate *within your own heart* that sets you free from any pain created by the conduct of others.

As the world continues to heal and evolve, it's so easy to focus on the injustice of everything, until you remember from a vibrational standpoint—love is what makes things right. When love is your liberator, it is a powerful, bold, and courageous shift to building an intimate relationship with your feelings. If I do not like the way life feels, let me love that part of myself. If I wish things were different, let me love the one who wishes for that. Let me not be a character waiting to be loved, but realize that *I am love,* materialized into physical form.

Any feeling of discord, anger, sadness, betrayal, heartbreak, hurt, abuse, abandonment—anything that dares to arise could only be begging for communion with the truth, beauty, and presence of your unconditional love. Feel into your heart, your body, what's begging for attention. Is it a memory? Is it a thought? Is it a fear? Is it a worry that time is running out?

In Golden Rule #10, we come upon a very important fork in the road, one that determines how much longer we spend in ego or how much time we spend communing as the soul. The question is: Do I continue playing out the character who's been hurt, or do I love the hurt within me as the love that liberates all?

LOVE BEGINS WITH HONESTY

Love begins with *honesty.* When you are loving, you are honest about your pain. Honesty brings attention to the parts that beg to remember its eternal wholeness. Like a processional line of emotions standing single file, they're waiting to be embraced by the light of their Source. That Source is none other than you. One by one, anger, sadness, jealousy, betrayal—all in line to be accepted, respected, honored, and admired—just as they are. Anger will never stop being angry. Hurt will never stop hurting. It's just waiting to be loved. We're not here to change the viewpoint of our experiences; we're here to *love* the experiences arising within us—even when the next one in line to be loved is the feeling of dislike. We are here to be the love that we are, and it starts with being honest with ourselves.

The soul knows that just by admitting how it feels, it's loosening the tension and allowing love to have an easier time healing each emotion. The ego is in a state of negotiation, trying to figure out why it feels this way and trying to negotiate into a different experience. In essence, the soul openly states what the ego debates. The ego asks, "Why do I feel so sad?" And the soul says, "Sadness is here to be loved."

Because we are one, all of what represents itself as your hurtful past is equally connected to the world's history of pain. Therefore, what is arising inside of your body, mind, and heart are all the patterns that love is liberating for humanity. Just as there is one eternal breath, and we are all the experience of how differently that one breath is being breathed, so every single thing you are doing for yourself is also what you're doing for the world. Through the art of letting go, you are liberated out of the pitfalls of victimhood, out of the agony of ego, and into the maturity of a fully integrated soul. When love is your liberator, as letting go occurs, you have become one less person who needs to be saved or rescued. This reveals one of the most important attributes of the soul: the power of unconditional love.

Based on the wisdom of Golden Rule #8, you don't have to like how anyone acts in order to see that love is what they need. Even if you're not in a position to offer the love that someone else needs, simply call upon the Universe that is always ready to work through you. Simply say, "I know this person needs love more than anything, but I'm unable to provide that. Universe, please send them the love I cannot give them." This is how the honesty of your personal experience allows you to be catalysts of healing in the lives of others without giving away your power or believing the fate of every person rests on your shoulders.

EXERCISE: Our Spiritual Pledge

As children, we stood up before class to do the Pledge of Allegiance. When was the last time you did that? When we place our hand on our heart, it is like taking a spiritual pledge.

In embracing the wisdom of the 10 Golden Rules, your spiritual pledge is:

"In this moment, I am pledging my allegiance to myself, to always be my ally, to never be an enemy, and to always be on my side. In order to be on my side, I cannot be against *anyone,* because the energy it takes to be against someone is time away from being there for me."

This is our spiritual pledge of allegiance to ourselves, to be one with our Source, and dedicated to living in service to the world we are healing together as one. Your past could have hurt you, it could have taken many things from you, but it can't take you away from yourself.

Through the beauty of a spiritual pledge of allegiance, you take the next step into unconditional love by asking your heart the question: What is it you need from me in order to be whole?

Maybe the words are "I'm sorry," or "I love you," or "I see you."

Maybe what your heart needs is "I like you. I see you. You're okay. I love you just as you are. I like the person you've become. I'm proud to be you."

Feel that last statement for a moment: I'm proud to be you. Those are the words that it took me almost 40 years to say with 100 percent conviction to myself: "Matt Kahn, I'm proud to be you." I've come so far in my journey; if there's an opportunity to incarnate again, I'm definitely coming back as me. That's how much fun I'm having now. It's the palpable guaranteed result of being liberated by love. It is both my living testimony and my invitation to you. Your willingness is life's only requirement.

YOUR MANTRA FOR RULE #10

When love is your liberator, you are allowing, on a subconscious level, for love to become more familiar and less foreign. This is a concept highlighted in my first book, *Whatever Arises, Love That.*

As I state in that book, there's a filing system in the subconscious mind, where there are categories of things that are familiar, based on the past, and foreign, based on how infrequently they've been experienced.

If you are someone who has not experienced unconditional love on a frequent basis, your subconscious mind puts it under the foreign category. This makes the ability to receive love seem daunting, overwhelming, and scary, even if there is a desire to be loved in your conscious mind. Thankfully, the solution is simple. The more familiar you become with unconditional love, the safer you are to receive it, whether coming directly from Source or the heart of another person.

Let's move unconditional love out of the foreign category of the subconscious mind to make love a more familiar experience for you to receive. Just place your hand on our heart, and with the utmost authenticity, repeat after me:

I love you.

If it feels weird, forced, or foreign, remember, it's just because unconditional love may not be something you have a point of reference for. You may have experienced love from others, but we are here to allow loving ourselves to be a more familiar experience. The more we introduce unconditional love to ourselves, the more trusting of life we become.

Try repeating this mantra for two minutes, slowly and openly:

I love you.

It may not have been easy for other people to love you, but it doesn't have to be hard for you to love yourself.

I love you.

The mind may say, okay, I get it, I love you, what's next?

I love you.

In order for love to be your liberator, you need to make time to love. Giving yourself exactly what you need. Sometimes, what you need is time to be more attentive with your feelings. Instead of trying to figure out what you feel and how to get beyond it, you need to just listen and be there with yourself—one breath at a time. Sometimes you may have been too entrenched in a spiritual journey and have gone from one self-help process to the next. In that case, the most loving thing is to give yourself a break from your own micromanagement. Sometimes, the love that you need is giving yourself a creative outlet to express your feelings, desires, and pain in creative, artistic ways. Sometimes, the love that you require is to be the kind of loving parent that you may not have had.

There are infinite ways to love yourself. All of which are important moments to be the constant reminder that no matter how life plays out, you are always on your side.

THREE SIMPLE INVITATIONS

In this moment, what is the very thing that you're willing to do differently to bring more love to your life? Is it taking the time to say to yourself the words that other people don't often say? Is it taking the time to point out the things you're doing right and not look at all the things you think you're doing wrong? Is it not making yourself such a spiritual project?

What are you willing to do differently *right now* to become more of love in form? Just for yourself. What are you willing to do differently, and how are you willing to *choose* differently, in order to become more of the love that you are? What needs to change in order for you to say *yes* to the liberation of letting go? What do you need to do in order, in this moment, to once and for all deem yourself worthy of love?

In love, there are three simple invitations. As you open to receive the three invitations, only more love will be given.

Invitation #1: Come as you are.
Invitation #2: Be as you wish.
Invitation #3: Feel it now.

Heaven has invited you to an important meeting. It says *come as you are.* Not once you're perfect, not when you have been stirred to your preferred and desired consistency; come as you are.

As you arrive at heaven's doorway what's the right way to act here? It's called *be as you wish.* Be as you wish, your choice. Be as you wish and *feel it now.* It, *I-T. I-T* stands for infinite truth. Feel infinite truth now, because the truth is that love is your liberator. It is what you are, as you become conscious of yourself as the Universe in human form.

Come as you are, be as you wish, feel it now.

Love is another name for God, Source, or the Universe. It is the infinite name of truth. Of all the names it goes by, my favorite name of truth—is you.

You are the love that liberates all.

Isn't it amazing when something so powerful erupts, it's like the world stops spinning? Everything just drops away. That's what happens when truth arrives, the moment you remember exactly who you are.

SPIRITUAL MYTH-BUSTING: "Life is an illusion."

It is clearer to say you are more than meets the eye than to suggest any illusion in existence. While you may have spent the majority of your life defending the character of a person, it doesn't mean you or anyone else has been tricked. When identifying with your personality, it is like knowing yourself as the center of a rainbow, unaware of all the many vivid layers around you. As you awaken in consciousness, your perception expands to know yourself not just as a person, but *an entire Universe of infinite possibility.* Life is not an illusion, because the word *illusion* infers something appearing to be the way it's not. If David Copperfield snaps his fingers and makes an elephant disappear, the illusion is that it looks to be nowhere in sight, despite the black curtain you can't see. Everything that looks the way it is exists exactly the way it appears—there's just always *more* to the story. When the light of awakening truly dawns, you are likely to discover the truth of existence living in form, expressing its perfection however you seem to be.

Since the word *illusion* means "something that is not"—because everything is an expression of truth, there is no such thing as an illusion. If illusion is something that is not, how are you going to find it? Anything found could only be what is, and to renounce anything that is could only be a clever form of denial. It's far more accurate to say everything is an expression of truth, and because everything is bound to change, such a truth only expands to be more vast, revealing, and inclusive. All that you believed in childhood may not be what you believe as an adult, but it wasn't *wrong* for you to believe all that you did before. Smaller truths are innocent building blocks creating foundations for bigger truths to be built. To say anything is an illusion is merely the ego's regret for having to crawl in order to walk.

The majority of the time a spiritual path leans hard in the direction of viewing life as an illusion, it is often as a way of bypassing the hardships of life and unresolved density of the emotional body. Because each awakening spirit must integrate into the physical body, the human experience is not something to get away from. No matter the strategy employed, anything rejected in the beginning of a spiritual journey must be faced and embraced in the end. This is why I teach in the most loving way. Because I know each and every thing you attempt to outrun will only be waiting for you at a later date.

The truth of life is that all is one. This doesn't make the perceived separateness of individual experience illusory in any way, since it is only the truth residing in form. If only the truth resides in form, then it is only the truth of all that chooses to be in form. If only the truth has chosen to be in form, then no illusion exists, with no one being tricked by anything in view.

Just because truths can only become *greater expressions* of truth doesn't mean any initial layer of truth was wrong or illusory to believe. You are far more than meets the eye, but you'll never truly get a felt sense of your ever-expanding trajectory trying to embrace a spiritual reality while renouncing the personal realm. Since the truth of life is always rooted in love, the nature of clarity is an all-inclusive truth uniting all individual expressions as equal aspects of Source. Each of us, no matter who we are or what we imagine we're not, are unique gems in the crown of heaven's kingdom. There's no reason to suggest any of the crown jewels are fake just to point toward or emphasize the reality of heaven's glory.

There is nothing illusory about you, your experiences, or the journey you're on. It took the utmost courage to come here and see each lifetime through, all within a vacuum of experiences, where only the reality of unconditional love can ever be revealed.

If illusion is anything, it is a word. So to say, life is an illusion, it's actually an incorrect statement. Life is a word suggesting whatever depth of a meaning such a word represents to you. Illusion is also a word. Suggesting life and illusion are both words is absolutely true, but to say life is an illusion remains a statement of belief and not a timeless fact. Life is not an illusion. Life is the word of divinity that comes to life in an intersection of time and space. To say it's an illusion denies the purpose of your existence. Without an illusion to find, everything could only be an existential miracle taking shape before you. With no illusion to blame for your life, there is only the magic of this very moment, an open-ended spectrum of inconceivable possibility that invites you across the threshold of limitation the moment you let go.

CONCLUSION

The Dawning of a New Era

No matter how the twists and turns of life may be, the 10 Golden Rules of letting go are always here to help you navigate the clearest, most heart-centered spiritual path. Each rule echoes the timeless truths that our one eternal Source always wishes for you to remember:

No matter what, you've done nothing wrong.

Anyone who blames you isn't happy.

Adversity can be fast-tracked through thankfulness.

Feeling better always helps everyone heal.

Well-being is a signal that you're ready to embody your potential.

The universe *always* has a plan.

While everything changes, it could only change you for the better.

In order to be emotionally free, it's okay to dislike.

But keep it balanced with creative expression, because projecting anger will drain you of energy.

Most of all, no matter what arises, no matter what comes and goes, it could only be the next part of ourselves to be loved, held, and adored, deeper than ever before, because love is your liberator.

These 10 Golden Rules outline your path, your purpose, and your mission. This is the dawning of a new era. It is the emergence of a new spiritual paradigm.

It is a brand-new beginning, where you are ready to return to your world, your family, and your relationship, more healed, transformed, and ready for life's most incredible adventure. Throughout every chapter, this book has prepared you for what is to come. It's not an illusion, but the greatest joy you've been seeking. It's ready to be birthed now that you've let go.

As always, it's been an honor to serve you.

May you be loved now and in all the days to come—from my heart to yours.

Until next time.

All for love,
Matt Kahn

ABOUT THE AUTHOR

Matt Kahn is the best-selling author of *Whatever Arises, Love That* and *Everything Is Here to Help You*. He is a spiritual teacher and highly attuned empathic healer who has become a YouTube sensation with his healing and often humorous videos.

Website: www.MattKahn.org

Hay House Titles of Related Interest

YOU CAN HEAL YOUR LIFE, the movie,
starring Louise Hay & Friends
(available as a 1-DVD program, an expanded 2-DVD set,
and an online streaming video)
Learn more at www.hayhouse.com/louise-movie

THE SHIFT, the movie, starring Dr. Wayne W. Dyer
(available as a 1-DVD program, an expanded 2-DVD set,
and an online streaming video)
Learn more at www.hayhouse.com/the-shift-movie

***

COMPENDIUM OF MAGICAL THINGS: Communicating with the Divine to Create the Life of Your Dreams, by Radleigh Valentine

IT'S NOT YOUR MONEY: How to Live Fully from Divine Abundance, by Tosha Silver

SUPER ATTRACTOR: Methods for Manifesting a Life beyond Your Wildest Dreams, by Gabrielle Bernstein

UNCHARTED: The Journey through Uncertainty to Infinite Possibility, by Colette Baron-Reid

All of the above are available at your local bookstore,
or may be ordered by contacting Hay House (see next page).

***

We hope you enjoyed this Hay House book. If you'd like to receive our online catalog featuring additional information on Hay House books and products, or if you'd like to find out more about the Hay Foundation, please contact:

HAY HOUSE

Published in India by:
Hay House Publishers (India) Pvt Ltd
Muskaan Complex, Plot No. 3,
B-2, Vasant Kunj, New Delhi 110 070
Phone: +91 11 41761620
www.hayhouse.co.in

Published in Australia by:
Hay House Australia Publishing Pty Ltd
18/36 Ralph St., Alexandria NSW 2015
Phone: +61 (02) 9669 4299
www.hayhouse.com.au

Published in the United Kingdom by:
Hay House UK Ltd
The Sixth Floor, Watson House,
54 Baker Street, London W1U 7BU
Phone: +44 (0) 203 927 7290
www.hayhouse.co.uk

Published in the United States of America by:
Hay House LLC
P.O. Box 5100, Carlsbad, CA 92018-5100
(760) 31-7695 or (800) 654-5126
www.hayhouse.com® • www.hayfoundation.org

'The gateways to wisdom and knowledge are always open.'

Louise Hay